New D

CW00661940

Edited by **Gordon Giles**   May–August 2023

7	**Ephesians 1—2** Matt McChlery	*1–6 May*
14	**Psalms 15—29** Elizabeth Rundle	*7–20 May*
29	**The upper room** Gordon Giles	*21–27 May*
37	**The sermon on the mount:** **Matthew 5—7** Veronica Zundel	*28 May–10 June*
52	**Mark 7—10** Michael Mitton	*11–24 June*
67	**1 Corinthians 11—14** Naomi Starkey	*25 June–8 July*
82	**Summer** Tim Heaton	*9–22 July*
97	**The road to Jerusalem** Tony Horsfall	*23 July–5 August*
112	**The temple** Lakshmi Jeffreys	*6–19 August*
127	**Micah** Amanda Bloor	*20–31 August*

15 The Chambers, Vineyard
Abingdon OX14 3FE
brf.org.uk

Bible Reading Fellowship is a charity (233280) and company
limited by guarantee (301324), registered in England and Wales

ISBN 978 1 80039 176 5
All rights reserved

Distributed in Australia by:
MediaCom Education Inc, PO Box 610, Unley, SA 5061
Tel: 1 800 811 311 | admin@mediacom.org.au

Distributed in New Zealand by:
Scripture Union Wholesale, PO Box 760, Wellington 6140
Tel: 04 385 0421 | suwholesale@clear.net.nz

Acknowledgements
Scripture quotations marked with the following abbreviations are taken from the
version shown. **NIV:** The Holy Bible, New International Version, Anglicised edition,
copyright © 1979, 1984, 2011 by Biblica. Used by permission of Hodder & Stoughton
Publishers, an Hachette UK company. All rights reserved. 'NIV' is a registered
trademark of Biblica. UK trademark number 1448790. **NRSV:** The New Revised
Standard Version of the Bible, Anglicised Edition, copyright © 1989, 1995 by the
Division of Christian Education of the National Council of the Churches of Christ
in the USA. Used by permission. All rights reserved. **GNT:** The Good News Bible
published by The Bible Societies/HarperCollins Publishers Ltd, UK © American
Bible Society 1966, 1971, 1976, 1992, used with permission. **NLT:** The Holy Bible,
New Living Translation, copyright © 1996, 2004, 2007, 2013. Used by permission of
Tyndale House Publishers, Inc., Carol Stream, Illinois 60188. All rights reserved.

A catalogue record for this book is available from the British Library

Printed by Gutenberg Press, Tarxien, Malta

Suggestions for using *New Daylight*

Find a regular time and place, if possible, where you can read and pray undisturbed. Before you begin, take time to be still and perhaps use the BRF prayer on page 6. Then read the Bible passage slowly (try reading it aloud if you find it over-familiar), followed by the comment. You can also use *New Daylight* for group study and discussion, if you prefer.

The prayer or point for reflection can be a starting point for your own meditation and prayer. Many people like to keep a journal to record their thoughts about a Bible passage and items for prayer. In *New Daylight* we also note the Sundays and some special festivals from the church calendar, to keep in step with the Christian year.

New Daylight and the Bible

New Daylight contributors use a range of Bible versions, and you will find a list of the versions used opposite. You are welcome to use your own preferred version alongside the passage printed in the notes. This can be particularly helpful if the Bible text has been abridged.

New Daylight affirms that the whole of the Bible is God's revelation to us, and we should read, reflect on and learn from every part of both Old and New Testaments. Usually the printed comment presents a straightforward 'thought for the day', but sometimes it may also raise questions rather than simply providing answers, as we wrestle with some of the more difficult passages of scripture.

New Daylight is also available in a deluxe edition (larger format). Visit your local Christian bookshop or BRF's online shop **brfonline.org.uk**. To obtain an audio version for the blind or partially sighted, contact Torch Trust for the Blind, Torch House, Torch Way, Northampton Road, Market Harborough LE16 9HL; +44 (0)1858 438260; **info@torchtrust.org**.

Comment on *New Daylight*

To send feedback, please email **enquiries@brf.org.uk**, phone **+44 (0)1865 319700** or write to the address shown opposite.

Writers in this issue

Amanda Bloor is archdeacon of Cleveland in the diocese of York, and has previously been a bishop's chaplain, a diocesan director of ordinands, an advisor in women's ministry and a parish priest. Her newest identity is that of grandmother, which gives her enormous pleasure.

Tim Heaton is a parish priest and rural dean of Blackmore Vale in the diocese of Salisbury. He is the author of the best-selling Lent course *The Long Road to Heaven* (Circle Books, 2013). You can connect with him at **facebook. com/lentcourses**.

Tony Horsfall is an author, retreat leader and mentor based in Bournemouth. He is married to Jilly, a counsellor, and between them they have four married children and six grandchildren. They are part of GodFirst church and share a passion to see people thrive in life and ministry.

Lakshmi Jeffreys is the rector of a parish just outside Northampton. She combines this with being a wife, mother, friend, dog-walker, school governor and various other roles, within and beyond the wider church.

Matt McChlery is an author, songwriter and an overseer at his local church. He has written numerous songs for the church and has penned three books, the most recent of which is *Standing in the Storm* (Instant Apostle, 2022), a memoir about his journey through non-Hodgkins lymphoma in 2016.

Michael Mitton works freelance in the areas of spirituality and mission. He is an honorary canon of Derby Cathedral and has written a number of books for BRF, including *Restoring the Woven Cord* (BRF, 2019).

Elizabeth Rundle has written many study and devotional books, including *20 Questions Jesus Asked* for BRF. She has written and presented scripts for local and national radio and television, and organised and led 16 pilgrimages to the Holy Land.

Naomi Starkey is a priest in the Church in Wales, based in a group of North Anglesey churches and also working more widely as a pioneer evangelist.

Veronica Zundel is an Oxford graduate, writer and columnist. She lives with her husband and son in North London. Her most recent book is *Everything I Know about God, I've Learned from Being a Parent* (BRF, 2013).

Gordon Giles writes...

This time last year Rochester Cathedral hosted *The Leaves of the Trees*, an artistic installation by Peter Walker. It comprised 5,000 metal leaves, spread on the ground, flowing down from – or ascending to – the high altar. At the altar the leaves were shiny stainless steel, whereas at the other end they were rusted and brown. Intended as a memorial to the thousands who died in the Covid-19 pandemic, each leaf had the word 'hope' engraved upon it. Many visitors came, some of whom took selfies in front of them, while others wept quietly in the presence of the representation of loss and hope.

The quietly rusting leaves were intended to remind us of the heavenly city, where 'the leaves of the tree are for the healing of the nations' (Revelation 22:2, NIV), and for many they spoke of healing in a post-pandemic world. Whoever we are, whatever we have done, whoever we have lost, there is hope engraved on the heart of our being, and this will bear us forward through thick and thin, rust and decay, love and loss. As Christina Rossetti put it, in her poem 'A Better Resurrection' (1862), 'My life is in the falling leaf: O Jesus, quicken me.'

It was then, as now, Eastertide. Rusting leaves remind us of autumn and the dying of the light, but at this time of year they are greening for spring and summer. Leaves green and then brown, reaching for light and then falling as the light fails. So we live in the moment of the here and now, with its memories, joys, sorrows and expectations. But we also mark the cycle of seasons and remember loved ones who have fallen, yet who are to be made shiny and new in the eternal, heavenly city.

Five years after Rossetti wrote her Easter poem, the hymn writer Walter Smith (1824–1908) gave us these lines:

> To all life thou givest, to both great and small;
> in all life thou livest, the true life of all;
> we blossom and flourish as leaves on the tree,
> and wither and perish but naught changeth thee.

Amid all the changes of the last year or so, in our monarchy, government and internationally, we know that in our changeless, loving, creator God we find resurrection hope revealed in Jesus Christ, our risen Lord.

REVD CANON DR GORDON GILES

The BRF Prayer

Faithful God,
thank you for growing BRF
from small beginnings
into a worldwide family of ministries.
We rejoice as young and old
discover you through your word
and grow daily in faith and love.
Keep us humble in your service,
ambitious for your glory
and open to new opportunities.
For your name's sake,
Amen

Helping to pay it forward

As part of our Living Faith ministry, we're raising funds to give away copies of Bible reading notes and other resources to those who aren't able to access them any other way, working with food banks and chaplaincy services, in prisons, hospitals and care homes.

If you've enjoyed and benefited from our resources, would you consider paying it forward to enable others to do so too?

Make a gift at **brf.org.uk/donate**

Ephesians 1—2

 Have you ever been in prison? I have. I wasn't locked up behind bars; I had been invited to help a friend of mine, who was a chaplain at a maximum-security prison near to where I live, conduct a church service one Sunday. Getting from the entrance to the chapel was quite a process: numerous checks and searches were conducted, then we were escorted through a winding system of corridors that had barred doors that needed to be unlocked and locked again every few metres. It was highly unpleasant, even though it was a modern and humane facility.

Paul wrote his letter to the Christians in Ephesus while he was imprisoned in Rome. I have no idea what prison was like for him. It is suggested that he was under house arrest, so conditions were perhaps a little more bearable than being shackled to a wall in a dark dungeon, but still fairly dismal. In a situation like this, unsure if the words he wrote would be his last, I assume he would want to make every word count.

Early manuscripts of this letter omit the phrase 'in Ephesus' (1:1), which gives rise to the suggestion that Paul was writing more generally to Christians everywhere rather than to a specific group or church. This is further reinforced by the fact that this letter does not address anyone by name nor deal with issues specific to a particular church, as other letters do. So, as we read this letter, let us remember that although these words were originally intended for a first-century audience, they can still be applied to our lives as believers in Jesus today.

Over the next week, I invite you to join me as we look at the first part of this remarkable letter. We will see how, as Christians, we are to view ourselves in our new-found position of being 'in Christ'; how we are to behave as children of God; and how we have been equipped and empowered by God to live the life he has called us to: a life that is only possible by the empowering of his Holy Spirit within us.

MATT MCCHLERY

We are family

Blessed be the God and Father of our Lord Jesus Christ, who has blessed us in Christ with every spiritual blessing in the heavenly places, just as he chose us in Christ before the foundation of the world to be holy and blameless before him in love. He destined us for adoption as his children through Jesus Christ, according to the good pleasure of his will, to the praise of his glorious grace that he freely bestowed on us in the Beloved.

If you approach the community centre where our church gathers on Sundays, you will see a large banner on the railings near the main entrance that says, 'We are family.' It is a bold statement. When we decided to create it, we wanted to say something that was welcoming and reflective of the nature of our church.

The phrase above is more than a catchy slogan on a banner; it reflects the heart of what Paul is speaking about in today's reading. God chose us long before we even thought about choosing him. He chose to love us despite our brokenness and dysfunction. He also chose to make us part of his family, the closest and most loving relationship possible. Relationship is extremely important to God. We are born into families because this is how God intended us to live, in loving relationship with one another.

So when we gather as a church, we are also gathering as the family of God. It is not simply a nice idea to be friendly or to make every effort to get along with those we are in relationship with; if they are fellow Christians, they are brothers and sisters – we are family, and God calls us to live in unity with each other. Perhaps we know of someone in God's family whom we don't get along with. Maybe we too need to follow God's example and choose to love, just as he chose to love us despite our weakness and failures. We are adopted into the same family. Let us love our brothers and sisters and, in so doing, glorify God.

Is there someone you need to ask God to help you to love better?

MATT MCCHLERY

Sealed

In Christ we have also obtained an inheritance, having been destined according to the purpose of him who accomplishes all things according to his counsel and will, so that we, who were the first to set our hope on Christ, might live for the praise of his glory. In him you also, when you had heard the word of truth, the gospel of your salvation, and had believed in him, were marked with the seal of the promised Holy Spirit; this is the pledge of our inheritance towards redemption as God's own people, to the praise of his glory.

For my 21st birthday, my parents had a special signet ring made for me. It had our family crest engraved on it. In the past, these rings were used to seal letters by pressing them into molten sealing wax, displaying the family mark as a sign to show who wrote the letter. It also helped to prove that the letter was genuine. The document then carried the weight of the family's reputation and associated power.

In Paul's day, a seal represented not only ownership, but also protection. Here, we are encouraged with the fact that from the moment we first believed in Jesus, we were marked with a seal that identifies us as one of God's children. That seal is the Holy Spirit, who not only marks us out as a Christian, but also gives us a taste of what life will be like in the future when we enter eternity – where sin will be no more, and we have new, recreated bodies as we live in God's presence forever. The presence of the Holy Spirit in our lives is a guarantee of our eternal inheritance in Christ.

Whatever you are facing in your life right now, know that, as a believer in Jesus, you are sealed with the Holy Spirit. You belong to Jesus, and he will be with you. He will protect you. Know that his promises will be fulfilled and one day, when all things are made new again, you will be with him forever.

Jesus, please remind me that I am yours. Remind me that my whole life belongs to you. Thank you for sending your Holy Spirit to help and to protect me. Amen

MATT MCCHLERY

Mighty power

I pray that the God of our Lord Jesus Christ, the Father of glory, may give you a spirit of wisdom and revelation as you come to know him, so that, with the eyes of your heart enlightened, you may know what is the hope to which he has called you, what are the riches of his glorious inheritance among the saints, and what is the immeasurable greatness of his power for us who believe, according to the working of his great power. God put this power to work in Christ when he raised him from the dead and seated him at his right hand in the heavenly places, far above all rule and authority and power and dominion, and above every name that is named, not only in this age but also in the age to come.

When electricity was first beginning to be understood hundreds of years ago, I do not think those early scientific pioneers could have imagined the profound global impact it would have on everyday life. Electricity can be incredibly powerful and, if harnessed correctly, can be used in a wide variety of applications, from powering the watch on my wrist to cooking food, lighting up dark streets and powering cars.

Paul's prayer is for those in the Ephesian church to begin to understand that they have received access to God's incomparable power. This is not just any power. It is the same mighty and miraculous power that raised Christ from the dead. This power is God's, and it wages war in the spiritual realms. It is the most powerful thing in existence.

God has delegated the access to and use of his power to those who believe. He is at work in us and through us. We need to administer the use of his power through the Holy Spirit wisely. We may think we are nothing special, but Jesus disagrees. He has given us the most powerful thing in the universe to help transform us to become more and more like him.

Like those early scientists, let us work at trying to better understand the power we have been given so that we can live lives that are pleasing to God.

Jesus, fill me with your power today. Amen

MATT MCCHLERY

Grace

You were dead through the trespasses and sins in which you once lived, following the course of this world, following the ruler of the power of the air, the spirit that is now at work among those who are disobedient. All of us once lived among them in the passions of our flesh, following the desires of flesh and senses, and we were by nature children of wrath, like everyone else. But God, who is rich in mercy, out of the great love with which he loved us even when we were dead through our trespasses, made us alive together with Christ – by grace you have been saved.

Have you heard the phrase 'random acts of kindness' before? It is when someone does something kind for someone else for no reason or reward, like paying for the person behind them at a drive-through restaurant or giving a bunch of flowers to a stranger.

Grace is similar to this, in that it is completely unwarranted and undeserved yet offered freely. Where the similarity diverges is that grace is not random. In fact, the grace God offers us is so intricately woven into his plan for our salvation; it is premeditated. It is because of God's immense love for us that he freely offers us his grace – an opportunity where we can choose his salvation. To be made alive despite the fact we were once spiritually dead in our sin.

Those of us who have been Christians for a long time can fall into the trap of thinking that some people are too far gone in their sin to be saved. Or perhaps we may have begun to see those who are not believers as being less worthy of God's love than us? Here we are reminded that we too were once just as sinful as everyone else – if God's grace was enough for us, surely it is enough for them also?

Let's not forget the beautiful gift of grace God freely offers. No matter how broken or undeserving we may feel, let us once again embrace the deliberate love shown to us through the death and resurrection of Jesus.

Jesus, I need your love and grace every day. Amen

MATT MCCHLERY

Called to do good

For by grace you have been saved through faith, and this is not your own doing; it is the gift of God – not the result of works, so that no one may boast. For we are what he has made us, created in Christ Jesus for good works, which God prepared beforehand to be our way of life.

Yesterday, Paul reminded us of our sinful beginnings, but he used that to highlight the amazing gift of saving grace offered to us through Jesus. In today's reading, Paul reinforces the fact that we are saved by grace alone, which comes from God and not by any act or good deed we do. We cannot buy or bribe our way into salvation. It is a free gift that we either choose to accept by believing in Jesus, or not.

Salvation is a beautiful act of re-creation by our creator God. Our spirit is completely transformed and reborn. Yes, thought patterns and habits may take a while to catch up, but we now have the God-empowered ability to change them. As we are changed to become more and more like Jesus, our behaviour follows suit and good works should begin to flow out from us to touch and affect the world around us. Salvation is not just for the benefit of the one who is saved, but also for the benefit of everyone whom that person meets.

We cannot be saved by doing good works, but Paul explains here that once we are saved, we are then called to do good works as a result of our salvation.

This talk of doing good works may make you feel that it is all going to be a lot of hard work and perhaps you feel that you are not up for it. Don't get too worried about whether or not you are able to do it. If you are in Christ, you have Jesus' spiritual power at work within you, equipping you with everything you need to live in a way that pleases him. Keep your eyes fixed on Jesus, and he will show you what to do as well as when and how to do it.

Ask Jesus how you can do good for someone today.

MATT MCCHLERY

Citizens

[Jesus] came and proclaimed peace to you who were far off and peace to those who were near; for through him both of us have access in one Spirit to the Father. So then you are no longer strangers and aliens, but you are citizens with the saints and also members of the household of God, built upon the foundation of the apostles and prophets, with Christ Jesus himself as the cornerstone. In him the whole structure is joined together and grows into a holy temple in the Lord; in whom you also are built together spiritually into a dwelling-place for God.

I was born in Zimbabwe, a landlocked nation south of the equator in Africa. I emigrated to the UK in 2003 and then spent seven years going through the naturalisation process to become a British citizen. At my citizenship ceremony, I swore allegiance to the Queen and signed a document which meant I was officially a citizen of Great Britain. This meant I was now entitled to all the rights and privileges that any citizen of the country had. It also came with a sense of belonging.

Just before today's verses in Ephesians, Paul explains how Jews and Gentiles are reunited in Christ. There is no longer any separation. Indeed, anyone who believes in Jesus is now a citizen of the kingdom of God and part of God's family.

Paul also uses the image of a building to illustrate how all believers are part of the whole family of God, each a living stone joined together and dependent upon each other. It is a building that is filled with the Holy Spirit and is where God dwells.

If you are a believer, you need to be connected to God's family, the church. Elsewhere in the Bible, we are encouraged not to neglect the habit of meeting together, because doing so helps us grow. Maybe you need to return to God's family today, or perhaps you are being called to extend the arm of friendship to welcome those on the edges of church into the family, as a full citizen of the kingdom of God.

Jesus, help me to function as a citizen of your kingdom. Amen

MATT MCCHLERY

Psalms 15—29

 The Hebrew poetry that we find in the book of Psalms is often referred to as the song book of the Bible – a collection of poems, prayers, outpourings of anguish, celebration and faith which have enhanced Jewish worship for nearly 4,000 years. Within the Christian Bible, 150 psalms have continued to hold a prominent place in worship.

Singing is our ancient and universal mode of communication. From the beginning of time, every part of life and worship has found expression in song. 'Moses and the Israelites sang… to the Lord' and 'Miriam sang to them' (Exodus 15:1, 21, NRSV). The apostle Paul wrote to believers to 'sing psalms, hymns and spiritual songs to God' (Colossians 3:16). Our Lord Jesus himself also sang, as we read in Mark's account of the last supper: 'When they had sung the hymn, they went out to the Mount of Olives' (Mark 14:26). Many believe they sang Psalms 113—118 and 136.

The heart of each of the psalms makes a direct approach to God, sometimes even a bitter *reproach* to God. We find every emotion – praise and joy, fear and doubt – as well as teaching and a good smattering of national history. These timeless emotions and subjects are understandable to every age and culture.

Over the next two weeks we shall consider Psalms 15—29, which are generally accepted by scholars as having their origin in Israel's iconic King David. His experience as a young shepherd, soldier, warrior-king, husband-with-a-wandering-eye and father give depth and authenticity to the poetry. However, we cannot look on this collection of Hebrew poetry with the idea that the author sat down to create a seamless sacred work. The whole section covers many years, and some appear disjointed, like interrupted thoughts with probably long intervals between their composition.

I pray that in some of these psalms you will feel God speaking directly to your situation. But don't be disillusioned if others feel like distant, ancient liturgy at odds with our received teaching of Jesus. In whatever way you approach these prayer poems, give a thought to the millions past and present who have heard, read and sung these words, gained comfort in hard times and been drawn closer to God.

ELIZABETH RUNDLE

Spiritual highway code?

O Lord, who may abide in your tent? Who may dwell on your holy hill? Those who walk blamelessly, and do what is right, and speak the truth from their heart; who do not slander with their tongue, and do no evil to their friends, nor take up a reproach against their neighbours; in whose eyes the wicked are despised, but who honour those who fear the Lord; who stand by their oath even to their hurt; who do not lend money at interest, and do not take a bribe against the innocent. Those who do these things shall never be moved.

These short verses contain perfect instructions for life. Imagine you are a pilgrim making your journey to Jerusalem for one, or all three, of the great Jewish festivals. Your forebears trudged with Moses in the wilderness, believing God dwelt in a tent. By the time of this psalm, the stone temple had been built on Mount Zion, and the 'holy hill' in Jerusalem was perceived as God's dwelling place. This was such a sacred place that serious examination of the heart and lifestyle was necessary before priests could allow people entry.

The psalm goes straight to the heart of personal conduct and relationship with God. Think of those verses as a catechism or creed, conveying principles by which all God-fearing people should live. When we apply them to our culture, we recognise the power in these brief sentences. These are aims and desires able to transform nations, communities, families and individuals. We all like to think we take this teaching seriously, yet how easy it is to condemn, to gossip, to renege on a promise or to let physical or emotional bribery beguile us.

Psalm 15 is short and to the point. Its format succinctly lays out rules for upright living which could easily be learned by heart. For those entering the temple, the verses were like a booster for the ten commandments, rules for being what Jesus would later term 'pure in heart' (Matthew 5:8). Spirituality and morality become inextricably linked. The living God requires worship from a true heart responding to divine presence in obedience and love.

Lord God of Abraham, Isaac and Jacob, help me pass the test of this psalm, so that all I do and say today may be true, kind and encouraging. Amen

ELIZABETH RUNDLE

Joy in the Lord

I bless the Lord who gives me counsel; in the night also my heart instructs me. I keep the Lord always before me… Therefore my heart is glad, and my soul rejoices; my body also rests secure. For you do not give me up to Sheol, or let your faithful one see the Pit… In your presence there is fullness of joy; in your right hand are pleasures forevermore.

What total trust in the Lord this represents: words that exude confidence and a contentment in what we would consider hard and perilous times. The verses remind me of a hymn written by Revd Charles Wesley (1707–88): 'My God, I am thine, what a comfort divine, what a blessing to know that my Jesus is mine!… In the heavenly lamb, thrice happy I am, and my heart it doth dance at the sound of his name.'

The 18th century in which Wesley wrote was also hard and perilous, and in our own time life is fragile too. Even in the most sophisticated and seemingly comfortable situations we have learned we can take nothing for granted. I find a touching simplicity in this psalm. Attributed to David, no one can be certain of its origin; nevertheless, it speaks with contemporary freshness across the centuries in the mystery and miracle of God-inspired scripture.

One day we will all reach the end of life, or rather the closure of life as we understand it. The psalm addresses this link between life and death in an uncomplicated manner. In life he has 'chosen' the Lord God above all other surrounding and competing gods and is content with his choice. What an example! He is secure each day in the Lord's presence, in this life and for eternity.

Both Peter, addressing the Pentecost crowds in Jerusalem (Acts 2:27–28), and Paul, when preaching in the Syrian synagogue in Antioch (Acts 13:35), quote this Psalm to underline Jesus' resurrection. In Hebrew minds, Sheol was a place below ground for the spirits of the dead, a nothingness. But here is faith that death is not an end; there is something more – joy in the eternal presence of God. Surely faith to make our hearts sing!

'I shall be safely sheltered with the one who loves me best'
('Underneath the Daisies' by Agnes Neale, 1849–92).

ELIZABETH RUNDLE

Prayer for help and protection

Hear a just cause, O Lord; attend to my cry; give ear to my prayer from lips free of deceit… I call upon you, for you will answer me, O God; incline your ear to me, hear my words. Wondrously show your steadfast love, O saviour of those who seek refuge from their adversaries at your right hand. Guard me as the apple of the eye; hide me in the shadow of your wings.

The other day I overheard someone referring to their friend's grandson. 'He's the apple of her eye,' they said, a phrase summing up the pinnacle of love and pride. If we delve deeper into the phrase in this psalm, we see that it is not a request for God to be proud of us; rather the word translated 'apple' originally meant 'pupil'. The pupil of our eye is the most vulnerable and precious area, the part to be protected at all costs. So we surmise David felt vulnerable and in need of help. He turned to God for protection. It is a human quirk that we are so much quicker to ask for help in times of trouble and need than to give thanks and praise when all is going well.

There are difficult lines in this psalm. It seems David is demanding God's attention and informing God that he, David, has justice on his side. He instructs God to 'rise up' and cruelly cut down 'the wicked' (v. 13) and his 'deadly enemies' (v. 9). Egotistical poetry? For sure, but a true reflection of how retaliation has a short fuse in the human heart. Remember that we are looking back at Old Testament behaviour when the survival of God's people was paramount. Therefore, it was acceptable to eliminate opponents.

Yet there is a beautiful symbol of God's protecting love, which combines ancient thought with our Lord Jesus and, perhaps, our own experience. Matthew records Jesus lamenting over Jerusalem (Matthew 23:37), saying he would like to have gathered people as a hen gathers her chicks under her wings. Such a tender illustration. Four other psalms and Moses' song (Deuteronomy 32:11) use the image of sheltering under God's 'wings'. This psalm reflects the age-old clash between human and divine nature.

Thank you, Lord, for those who have sheltered me with love and tenderness. Amen

ELIZABETH RUNDLE

Song of triumph

I love you, O Lord, my strength. The Lord is my rock, my fortress, and my deliverer, my God, my rock in whom I take refuge, my shield, and the horn of my salvation, my stronghold. I call upon the Lord, who is worthy to be praised; so I shall be saved from my enemies… The Lord lives! Blessed be my rock, and exalted be the God of my salvation.

Hold on for a roller-coaster charge through King David's battles. No doubt these were actual battles as well as trials and tribulations in his life in general. This is soldiers' poetry, sprinkled with words like 'rock', 'shield', 'fortress' and 'stronghold', a song born out of war, praising God who had delivered victory. Considering the ravines and hostile areas in which David fought, there was no better way of depicting God's protection. Using powerful imagery, 'snares of death', 'torrents of perdition', 'quaking mountains', 'hailstones' and 'coals of fire', this man had lived through trauma. We sense his relief that, against all odds, God his rock has delivered him. Unlike the gods of surrounding nations, the God of Israel is a living presence!

In the nearly eight decades since the end of World War II, British forces have been deployed in more than 18 areas of the world. Every family, whichever side they may be on, prays for victory. Everyone involved in conflict longs for a deliverer, and the brutality expressed in some verses, however reprehensible to us, finds resonance in all battles. In human relationships, we all know what it means when we hear a person referred to as 'my rock'.

Thus we recognise the sentiments here as David rejoiced at his victory over Saul's army, and we can almost feel his sighs of relief and gratitude: 'It is over. I've got through it. Thanks be to God!'

Reading these lines you may recall coming through a personal dilemma, perhaps ill-health you have needed to fight against or an internal battle of the mind. On reaching five years since my surgeries for thyroid cancer, I look back with the words of an old German hymn:

'The Lord is never far away… an ever-present help and stay… our peace and joy and blessing… To God all praise and glory'
(Johann Schütz, 1640–90). Amen

ELIZABETH RUNDLE

The glory of God in creation

The heavens are telling the glory of God; and the firmament proclaims his handiwork… the fear of the Lord is pure, enduring forever; the ordinances of the Lord are true and righteous altogether. More to be desired are they than gold, even much fine gold… Let the words of my mouth and the meditation of my heart be acceptable to you, O Lord, my rock and my redeemer.

I am fortunate to spend several weeks in the summer at a caravan site in Devon. Far away from light pollution, I have been known to lie back and gaze into a clear night sky. There is something majestic in glimpsing stars, planets and the edge of our universe. The mathematical consistency of the solar system and the grandeur of what our eyes can see is breathtaking, let alone the greater visions to be revealed by the new, enormous James Webb space telescope, launched by NASA in 2021. We may call ourselves advanced, but we still echo the psalmist's words: the heavens are telling the glory of God, and we are lost in praise and wonder.

I like to think of Jesus with his disciples staring up into the night sky and recalling this psalm. Verses 3 and 4 present profound truth – beyond language, the sky 'speaks' to every nation and to each individual whatever their age. God's law, his ordinances, are indeed perfect. The sun rises in the morning regardless of what has happened on earth and the moon passes through its phases with unerring accuracy. How privileged we are to glimpse the almighty power and glory of the creator, of our creator.

The psalm goes on to equate the laws of creation with God's commandments for human communities. There are no better precepts by which we can live in peace and cooperation.

Many of us are familiar with the last verse of Psalm 19 perhaps without realising its origin. From the minds of great philosophers and preachers to our own snatched meditations, we use those words as we strive to make our thoughts and prayers acceptable to our creator. We cannot offer God half-hearted praise, but hearts that are humble, contrite and thankful.

'Glory to the Father, glory to the Son, and to Thee, blest Spirit, whilst all ages run' (Sabine Baring-Gould, 1834–1924).

ELIZABETH RUNDLE

A prayer for blessing?

May the Lord answer you when you are in distress; may the name of the God of Jacob protect you. May he send you help from the sanctuary and grant you support from Zion. May he remember all your sacrifices and accept your burnt offerings… Some trust in chariots and some in horses, but we trust in the name of the Lord our God. They are brought to their knees and fall, but we rise up and stand firm.

Is this psalm a prayer, a blessing or a battle hymn? Which words leap from David's heart to my own circumstances? I love to spread a newspaper over the table and devour columns of international events and characters. I am writing these notes in the wake of a World Day of Prayer. The world, God's wonderful world gifted to humans to nurture, lies riven with hatred, bloody wars and countless potential flash points for tragedy.

From the beginning of time has it ever been different? People have said to me they do not read the Old Testament because it is too gruesome. They cannot cope with all the battles and brutality of ancient times. If we look at Psalm 20 as a battle hymn, we see how the people looked to the God of Jacob to give them victory.

The more I read these words, the deeper and more meaningful they appear. Whatever the origin of this Hebrew poetry, it has a miraculous ability to inspire and comfort successive generations. How natural to pray that those we love may be comforted in distress; how normal to long for protection from the world's hostilities. Small or large, victories and achievements bring spontaneous gestures of joy. We can empathise with the emotions behind this poetry.

Then comes the blazing statement of faith. Some people put their trust in military force, but the psalmist puts their whole trust in God (v. 7). Look around the world today and see what happens when leaders put their trust in power and domination. Crushing military might leaves no room for love and peace. If you are stressed today by events around the world or anxieties at home, trust in the peace of God that we find in Jesus Christ.

'We have heard a joyful sound, Jesus saves, Jesus saves!'
(Priscilla Jane Owens, 1829–1907). Thanks be to God. Amen

ELIZABETH RUNDLE

Ever-present God

Your hand will find out all your enemies; your right hand will find out those who hate you… the Lord will swallow them up in his wrath, and fire will consume them. You will destroy their offspring from the earth… If they plan evil against you, if they devise mischief, they will not succeed. For you will put them to flight; you will aim at their faces with your bows. Be exalted, O Lord, in your strength! We will sing and praise your power.

Trigger warning: violent words of revenge. This psalm is supposed to be a song of thanksgiving for one of King David's victories, yet to our ears it sounds more like vindictive gloating. Deep within the human psyche, we have to admit, lurks a delight in seeing an opponent thrashed, whether in the extremes of war or in sports like rugby or football. Dominance has dangerous siblings in vengeance and retribution. The honesty of this psalm probes deep-seated attitudes and prejudices under the guise of piety and thanksgiving.

The world of the 21st century witnesses the same evils known since the birth of humanity – evils that feed on hatred, distrust, envy, greed and violence. And over time, leaders, often even great leaders, have claimed God's protection for themselves and become cheerleaders for the downfall and destruction of their enemies. The threat of vicious intent can feel unsettling. On the other hand, after the bloodthirsty phrases declaring God will destroy the king's enemies, the psalm ends on a note of praise.

Consider the areas of conflict in the world today. Or think about the crimes we all read about but seem powerless to eradicate – the prevalence of domestic violence, cruelty towards children and city stabbings. We must never underestimate the power of evil, but neither must we underestimate the power of God to transform and save. In his book *Psalms Now*, Leslie F. Brandt gives this translation of Psalm 21: 'I raise my voice in praise, O God, because no one can separate me from you.' That's certainly a thought to highlight. Does it remind you of Paul's words at the end of Romans 8? Can we repeat: nothing can separate us from the love of God in Jesus Christ our Lord.

Lord, when I rant and rave, help me to remember your goodness and love.

ELIZABETH RUNDLE

Triumphant prophecy

All the ends of the earth shall remember and turn to the Lord; and all the families of the nations shall worship before him. For dominion belongs to the Lord, and he rules over the nations… Posterity will serve him; future generations will be told about the Lord, and proclaim his deliverance to a people yet unborn, saying that he has done it.

Jesus quoted the opening lines of this psalm as he hung on the cross: 'My God, my God, why have you forsaken me?' (v. 1). Do we think that Jesus actually felt God had abandoned him? Or may this fragment of scripture from a dying man, struggling for breath as crucifixion slowly asphyxiated him, be a spontaneous repetition of this famous psalm? Was this sacred text going through our Lord's tortured mind as he forced his memory to keep focused? There are some amazing phrases which we do not often consider: 'since my mother bore me you have been my God' (v. 10); 'all my bones are out of joint; my heart is like wax' (v. 14); 'my mouth is dried up… and my tongue sticks to my jaws' (v. 15); 'a company of evildoers encircles me' (v. 16); 'they divide my clothes among themselves, and for my clothing they cast lots' (v. 18); 'deliver my soul from the sword' (v. 20). The resonance with Jesus hanging on the cross is heart-stopping.

Then from such oppressive gloom breaks forth the triumphant burst of prophecy. Through modern communications and the power of the Holy Spirit, all nations now have the means to hear about Jesus Christ.

'He has done it' are the words closing the psalm (v. 31). Does this remind you of the final words our Lord uttered as his earthly life came to a close? 'He said, "It is finished"' (John 19:30). The Greek word *tetelestai* has a far more rounded definition than simply 'finished' – it means not only a task completed or accomplished, but also *successfully* accomplished, the satisfactory fulfilment of the mission. So we should look on the final words of Jesus not as a cry of exhaustion and defeat but one of victory, a victory to be told and retold for the rest of time. God's purpose is to lift humanity from despair to hope; death will not be the end. Hallelujah!

Lamb of God, have mercy. Lamb of God, grant me peace. Amen

ELIZABETH RUNDLE

The tender love of God

The Lord is my shepherd, I shall not want. He makes me lie down in green pastures; he leads me beside still waters; he restores my soul. He leads me in right paths for his name's sake. Even though I walk through the darkest valley, I fear no evil; for you are with me; your rod and your staff – they comfort me.

At the 2021 RHS Chelsea Flower Show, a gold medal was awarded to the Bible Society-sponsored garden based on this much-loved psalm. Designed for the Sanctuary Garden category, the Psalm 23 garden had boulders placed so effectively they appeared to have been in situ forever. A waterfall, reminiscent of sudden cascades in the Judean desert, dropped into a soothing pool. Cool green vegetation surrounded the rocks and water creating a calm, reflective and safe space. It was a stunning design by Sarah Eberle.

Doctors and psychologists, magazines and TV shows enthusiastically promote the countryside for physical and mental well-being. The rediscovery of the benefits of the outdoors is now heralded as something to restore our equilibrium. City farms and rural retreats offer children and adults alike the chance to ground themselves with nature, both animal and vegetable.

If correctly attributed to King David, the words of this pastoral psalm were born from experience and speak from his heart to our hearts across centuries. Here was a man who had been a shepherd in his youth. He knew his sheep were totally dependent on him. The shepherd was in control. Sheep are frightened by gushing water, they can fall and be injured if they take the wrong path, and they need to find food. These are not unrealistic sentiments; they address our basic, timeless needs. In biblical times shepherds led their sheep. Nowadays shepherds in jeeps round up thousands of their flock. This psalm reminds us of an intimacy between shepherd and sheep. Jesus knows us by name. As we say this psalm, we affirm our dependence on Jesus, the good shepherd (John 10:11).

'O Jesus, shepherd, guardian, friend, my prophet, priest, and king,
my lord, my life, my way, my end, accept the praise I bring'
(John Newton, 1725–1807).

ELIZABETH RUNDLE

Comfort and confidence

You prepare a table before me in the presence of my enemies; you anoint my head with oil; my cup overflows. Surely goodness and mercy shall follow me all the days of my life, and I shall dwell in the house of the Lord my whole life long.

When I was a small child, before setting off from London to Cornwall on holiday, my family and I would always recite Psalm 23 (from the King James Version). Although I was I undoubtedly impatient to get going, sitting in the back seat of the car, nevertheless those words have stayed with me all my life. I blush to admit it remains the only psalm I know by heart! In the hymn book I grew up with, the setting of this psalm was number 50, and when I entered theological college to train for ministry, my room number was 50. After the death of my husband, these words began many a solo journey.

Set to the tune of 'Crimond', 'The Lord's my shepherd' has been an oft-chosen hymn at funerals for as long as I can remember. We cannot begin to imagine how many millions of people have found comfort in these words. David was not alone in his battles and flights from Saul; neither are we alone in our valleys of shadows and the battles we face.

The shadow of death was real to the composer of this psalm as well as to the composer of 'Crimond'. Jessie S. Irvine was 35 when she composed the tune and only 51 when she died in Scotland in 1887. The Bible tells us that King David was 30 when he became king and that he reigned for 40 years – 'a good age', everyone under 70 says! Today we can draw from these words the idea that even in the worst of all situations, death, we do not need to be afraid nor feel isolated, because God is with us. Then, ultimately, we will be in the presence of God for eternity. This is such a personal psalm – 'my' shepherd, 'you are with me'.

Lord, help me to remember that nothing is going to happen to me today that you and I together cannot handle.

ELIZABETH RUNDLE

A song of worship and welcome

The earth is the Lord's and all that is in it, the world, and those who live in it… Who shall ascend the hill of the Lord?… Those who have clean hands and pure hearts, who do not lift up their souls to what is false, and do not swear deceitfully. They will receive blessing from the Lord… Lift up your heads, O gates!… that the King of glory may come in.

This psalm sometimes seems to be two psalms fitted somewhat awkwardly together. Beginning as a creation poem acknowledging divine sovereignty, it continues with the moral requirements for living in God's fabulous world. Then the whole tone changes at verse 7 as worshippers enter a responsive song to welcome 'the King of glory!' This phrase is repeated five times, giving rise to the assumption that from verse 7 we are looking at a kind of temple hymn.

We can be sure this was a psalm sung at the temple in Jerusalem, because 'hill of the Lord' and 'holy place' represent Mount Zion, on which the temple was built. As we saw in Psalm 15, not everyone would be welcome: only those who followed the precepts of the law given to Moses. Worshippers were expected to be honest, honourable and sincere in their faith. Only then could they welcome the king of glory – not the nation's king but God himself. The temple was a sacred place of expectation, joy and praise, awaiting God's Messiah.

Many of us will remember that when Queen Elizabeth II travelled anywhere, she was met by crowds waving and chanting, and the same has been true for King Charles more recently. Often those who are honoured to meet the monarch are chosen for their upright life and charitable works. How much more meaningful, uplifting and inclusive should our lives and worship be for the king of glory.

We are truly blessed by music. Special occasions are made memorable by music and, as someone once said to me, 'Words speak to the mind, but music speaks to the soul.' Thank God that he gifted David with poetry and music that we too can lift our hearts to the king of glory.

'King of glory, king of peace, I will love thee… Wherefore with my utmost art, I will sing thee' (George Herbert, 1593–1633).

ELIZABETH RUNDLE

Prayer for guidance

Make me to know your ways, O Lord; teach me your paths. Lead me in your truth, and teach me, for you are the God of my salvation… Do not remember the sins of my youth… All the paths of the Lord are steadfast love and faithfulness… Turn to me and be gracious to me, for I am lonely and afflicted. Relieve the troubles of my heart, and bring me out of my distress.

This psalm shows us that even the king felt lonely and depressed by the ailments of age. We can picture King David, mature in years, finding that age has robbed him of many friends and brought physical 'afflictions' he never dreamed of in his youth. Oh, his younger self! Well, yes, he would rather God forgot about certain things he did in his youth. That could probably be said of all of us. Yet David turns to God for direction.

I'm reminded of seeing a three-armed ceramic signpost pointing towards 'Here', 'There' and 'Everywhere'. Pause to look at the paths you take each day. Perhaps most of your paths are 'Here', based around home and community. Other paths lead you 'There', for work, hospital, visiting relatives, journeys outside our home territory. Many will have followed the paths to 'Everywhere', tried many things, been to various places.

Perhaps you are thinking of your spiritual path with potholes of doubt and disappointment, ambitions curbed or the uphill struggle with depression. Does your path wind into uncharted alleys or lead you forward smoothly on an open road? King David was honest before God: things were getting on top of him, and he was lonely. Many say that the scourge of this age is loneliness. This is very sad when there has never been a time of such easy, instant communication. There is no easier communication than prayer.

So often we don't want anyone to know how much we are struggling, but God knows. His signpost points to the open arms of our Saviour Jesus Christ, leading us from where we are to where we need to be – restored, forgiven and loved.

'Guide me, O thou great redeemer, pilgrim through this barren land.
I am weak, but thou art mighty, hold me with thy powerful hand'
(William Williams, 1717–91).

ELIZABETH RUNDLE

Confidence

The Lord is my light and my salvation; whom shall I fear? The Lord is the stronghold of my life; of whom shall I be afraid?... Though an army encamp against me, my heart shall not fear; though war rise up against me, yet I will be confident... If my father and mother forsake me, the Lord will take me up... Wait for the Lord; be strong, and let your heart take courage; wait for the Lord!

King David was having a good day; the rhythm of this psalm has the drumbeat of confidence. You can almost hear trumpets blowing and choirs singing great anthems of praise. On my bookshelf I have a small pottery lamp from the village of Nazareth in the Holy Land. It is a humble little container for oil and wick, just like the ones Jesus' mother Mary would have used. Back in those days, the only light available came from the sun, from flames, lamps and candles, or, for a few days in the month, the moon. Light and dark were synonymous with good and evil, God's presence and human ignorance. Today we accept that people with seasonal affective disorder feel a whole lot better when the sun shines. Light was God's first gift in creation, and light is the main source of energy for all living organisms. You cannot get much more vital than that! So this psalm is not merely uplifting Hebrew poetry; it is a statement of daily faith.

As I write these notes, I admit a certain envy for David's positivity. In too many places in our glorious but hurting world, an army will have a threatening encampment and, I ask myself, if an army encircled my city, town or home, could I honestly say, 'My heart shall not fear'? War brings out both the best and the worst in human nature. My eyes often fill with tears at stories of great heroism and unstinting selflessness, the horror of wasted lives and ruined opportunities.

Through his wars, physical and spiritual, David looked to the Lord for strength, protection and victory. Take some time today to pause and take courage in the presence of Jesus Christ, the light of the world.

Lord, be my light today. Amen

ELIZABETH RUNDLE

The supremacy of God

Ascribe to the Lord, O heavenly beings, ascribe to the Lord glory and strength. Ascribe to the Lord the glory of his name; worship the Lord in holy splendour. The voice of the Lord is over the waters… the Lord sits enthroned as king forever. May the Lord give strength to his people! May the Lord bless his people with peace!

Amid all the battle references and cries for vengeance, again and again the poet stresses God's creative power. Some of our best-loved hymns and songs proclaim the power and glory of God: 'How great thou art' comes to mind, as does a children's action song, 'Our God is a great big God'. Whether the vastness of the sea, the magnificence of forests, the power of fire or the unfathomable heavens, these prayer poems declare that our God reigns. Despite all our material advances and conveniences, the elemental power and glory of nature still cause a gasp of wonder. It is awesome!

To me the interconnectedness of scripture is exciting and inspiring. To mention the 'voice of the Lord over the waters' is to refer directly to the creation account in Genesis 1. Equally important is the gospel story of Jesus calming the storm (Mark 4:39). The voice of Jesus brought calming peace over turbulent water.

Here the psalmist conveys an awe of God which we may have forgotten. Brilliant scientists have split the atom, equally brilliant astronomers reckon they are on the brink of finding the birth of our universe, and unimaginable wonders are researched in medicine and technology. This psalm puts God at the head and heart of all creation. Our lives are full of 'things' – as with over-cluttered homes we need to take a long, hard look at all we put before God.

Concluding these reflections on this group of psalms, let us endorse the psalmist's longing for peace, among nations, communities, churches, neighbours and families. And for each one of us, peace in our own hearts.

Dear Lord, when technology threatens to rule my days, help me to make time to marvel at the intricate beauty of blossom, the miracle of sunrise and the joy of human love. In these blessings may I find my joy and peace. Amen

ELIZABETH RUNDLE

The upper room

 After Ascension Day (18 May) we look forward to Pentecost, the day on which God sent the Holy Spirit to Jesus' disciples gathered in the upper room. In many churches, the post-ascension period is marked with a festival of mission and ministry known as 'Thy Kingdom Come'. It is an ecumenical movement of prayer and celebration which presents all sorts of creative opportunities for sharing the gospel and celebrating our faith, inside and beyond the church walls.

Just as the disciples gathered in their upper room at key moments in their shared lives – sometimes with Jesus, sometimes without – their calling to be together in that place was mirrored by a 'sending out' from there to preach, teach, heal and care for others. The upper room was their headquarters, the powerhouse in which they gathered, hid, prayed and prepared.

Sometimes we do not make the connections. We do not fully appreciate the sequence of events that took place under that space, and we do not, for example, always remember that the last supper, the appearance of Jesus to Thomas, the election of Matthias and the flames of Pentecost all occurred in the same space. That makes it a place of extreme fear, grief, joy and anticipation.

Many houses had 'upper' rooms, built on the flat roof of a typical Hebrew house or sometimes on a third storey. When Eutychus fell out of a window while Paul was speaking, he fell three storeys (Acts 20:9). Ahaziah also has a fatal fall from an upper room (2 Kings 1:2). Upper rooms are dangerous places, precariously placed between the realms of life and death. Elijah carries the widow of Zarephath's son to an upper room to raise him (1 Kings 17:19–23), and David goes to one to mourn Absalom (2 Samuel 18:33). In the New Testament, Dorcas is taken to an upper room when she dies, and it is where Peter goes to pray for her restoration (Acts 9:36–41).

As we enter this week of pre-Pentecost preparation, we might also reflect on whether there is an 'upper room' for God in ourselves: the space in our heads that welcomes and believes in divine salvation, brought about and ministered to us by the birth, life, death, resurrection and ascension of Jesus Christ, whose Spirit dwells uppermost in our lives even to this day.

GORDON GILES

Room for supper

So Jesus sent Peter and John, saying, 'Go and prepare the Passover meal for us that we may eat it.' They asked him, 'Where do you want us to make preparations for it?' 'Listen,' he said to them, 'when you have entered the city, a man carrying a jar of water will meet you; follow him into the house he enters and say to the owner of the house, "The teacher asks you, 'Where is the guest room, where I may eat the Passover with my disciples?'" He will show you a large room upstairs, already furnished. Make preparations for us there.' So they went and found everything as he had told them; and they prepared the Passover meal.

The twelfth-century Cenacle in Jerusalem claims to be the site of the upper room where the last supper took place. The name comes from the Latin *cenaculum* meaning 'dining room'. (*Cena*, in Latin and Italian, means 'evening meal'.) Even if we cannot be sure exactly where it is, the idea that the upper room still exists – and can be visited – is an alluring one.

The last supper was a pivotal event in history, an ending and a beginning. No passover had ever been like it before or would ever be again. It was depicted by Leonardo da Vinci in the late 1490s in the *Ultima Cena*, which is on display at the Cenacolo Vinciano in Milan. For conservation and space reasons, only 33 people are allowed in the room: one for each year of Jesus' earthly life. It was controversially used by Dan Brown in his novel *The Da Vinci Code*, but it is more notable for the fact it sets the supper in the costume of its day.

That final meal stands at the crossroads of new and old testaments, as Jesus takes the cup and bread, relates them to himself and invites all who follow him to re-enact and re-embody his physical and spiritual action in daily life thereafter. We still do it our day, and Christ is still with us, as we share in Holy Communion.

Be present, Jesus, that bread and wine may be to us your body and blood. Amen

GORDON GILES

Room service

[Jesus] got up from the table, took off his outer robe, and tied a towel around himself. Then he poured water into a basin and began to wash the disciples' feet and to wipe them with the towel that was tied around him. He came to Simon Peter, who said to him, 'Lord, are you going to wash my feet?' Jesus answered, 'You do not know now what I am doing, but later you will understand.' Peter said to him, 'You will never wash my feet.' Jesus answered, 'Unless I wash you, you have no share with me.' Simon Peter said to him, 'Lord, not my feet only but also my hands and my head!'

The first time we 'enter' the upper room is at the last supper. The first room shall be the last room, and vice versa! The room service there is heavenly. This service embodies Jesus' maxim that the 'first will be last, and the last will be first' (Matthew 19:30). In Luke's account of the last supper, Jesus says, 'But I am among you as one who serves' (Luke 22:27), and although Luke does not recount the foot washing, Jesus' statement sums it up.

Jesus treats his friends as royal guests, crawling on the ground before them to rinse dust and dirt off and then dry their feet. It is a manner of calling: just as he says, 'Do this in remembrance of me' in breaking bread, it is 'do as I do'. The man who is king serves those whom he is calling into service.

In the final week of Jesus' earthly ministry and the weeks thereafter, this upper room became a safe and sacred place for the apostles. They retreat to it after the crucifixion to hide, it is there that Jesus breathes on them the Holy Spirit and reveals himself to Thomas (John 20:19–29), and it is where they elect Matthias to succeed the traitor Judas (Acts 1:15–26). Thus there is a connection in this place between Jesus' sacrificial service and his mission, between his physical suffering and the spiritual outpouring which follows the resurrection. Wherever and whatever the upper room was, it is a significant place of calling and service.

Call me, Jesus, into spiritual and physical service. Amen

GORDON GILES

Room for peace

When it was evening on that day, the first day of the week, and the doors of the house where the disciples had met were locked for fear of the Jews, Jesus came and stood among them and said, 'Peace be with you.' After he said this, he showed them his hands and his side. Then the disciples rejoiced when they saw the Lord. Jesus said to them again, 'Peace be with you. As the Father has sent me, so I send you.' When he had said this, he breathed on them and said to them, 'Receive the Holy Spirit. If you forgive the sins of any, they are forgiven them; if you retain the sins of any, they are retained.'

The second part of John's description of Easter Day is often overlooked or saved up for a week later in church. First comes the garden scene, when Mary Magdalene finds the tomb empty and fetches John and Peter, who go home quickly (John 20:10). Mary remains, meets and eventually recognises Jesus and then, as the 'apostle to the apostles' as she is sometimes known, she rushes back to the upper room to tell the others that she has 'seen the Lord' (v. 18). Imagine her returning and knocking on the firmly locked door. Was there a special lockdown knock so they would know it was her?

During the periods of lockdown in 2020, this passage took on a special dimension as we recognised that the disciples were in isolation and locked behind closed doors, fearful and uncertain. We are the first generation in a long time to understand this. Yet there have always been people who lock themselves away and do not answer the door, frightened or avoiding the authorities, whether innocent or guilty.

Yet Jesus can get behind closed doors and share the peace. He understands our fear, and he transcends it, offering spiritual gifts of love, fellowship and peace. This pastoral empowerment is ours to have and hold and share. For he not only brings, but also sends. The need for peace and compassion is universal and always needed. We are the ones whose hands, feet, voices and touch can minister that peace to anyone whose hearts are locked in fear, shame or despair.

God, give me grace to share your love and mercy. Amen

GORDON GILES

Room for faith

A week later his disciples were again in the house, and Thomas was with them. Although the doors were shut, Jesus came and stood among them and said, 'Peace be with you.' Then he said to Thomas, 'Put your finger here and see my hands. Reach out your hand and put it in my side. Do not doubt but believe.' Thomas answered him, 'My Lord and my God!' Jesus said to him, 'Have you believed because you have seen me? Blessed are those who have not seen and yet have come to believe.'

I wonder how these cooped-up Christians-to-be handled the emotional and spiritual pressure that was in that upper room on that first Easter Day. Thomas had gone out when Jesus first appeared to them. Had he braved the lockdown to go and get supplies or to get some fresh air? What was that intervening week of doubt like?

History and culture know him as 'doubting Thomas', but we should call him 'believing Thomas'. Someone who scores the winning goal is known after the match as 'goal-scorer Bloggs, who in the 33rd minute netted a perfect curling free kick'. Though Bloggs did not score a goal before that 33rd minute, no one would call him 'non-scorer Bloggs, who left the pitch covered in mud', would they? No, they would call him 'goal-scorer Bloggs' or even 'man of the match'. So let us not call Thomas 'doubting'. Is he not the man of the match?

Thomas' goal was to verify his fellow disciples' claims – to believe in the depth of his heart and understand in the upper room of his head. He is gifted the opportunity to do so, which, on behalf of us all, he takes. The others don't believe immediately when Mary Magdalene tells them, or they rush to the tomb to check, or they are present when Jesus appears. Jesus asks Thomas whether he believes because he has seen, which after all is what the others have all done.

What Thomas does next is most important – having verified, he worships. For him evidence leads to faith, which leads to understanding, which leads to worship, as he exclaims, 'My Lord and my God!' (v. 28).

Jesus, verify my faith that I may worship you in Spirit and in truth. Amen

GORDON GILES

Prayer room

Then they returned to Jerusalem from the mount called Olivet, which is near Jerusalem, a sabbath day's journey away. When they had entered the city, they went to the room upstairs where they were staying, Peter, and John, and James, and Andrew, Philip and Thomas, Bartholomew and Matthew, James son of Alphaeus, and Simon the Zealot, and Judas son of James. All these were constantly devoting themselves to prayer, together with certain women, including Mary the mother of Jesus, as well as his brothers.

I served my curacy at the Church of the Good Shepherd in Cambridge, where the side chapel is dedicated to Nicholas Ferrar, the founder of the Little Gidding Community near Huntingdon. It has glass doors beautifully engraved with some words from T.S. Eliot's poem 'Little Gidding'.

As we move from the gospel accounts of Jesus' resurrection appearances to Acts, we notice a shift: in the upper room, where Thomas verified his faith and then worshipped Jesus, we now find the disciples praying together.

As Jews, they were permitted to travel only 2,000 cubits (three-quarters of a mile) on the sabbath. So they would have found themselves in the upper room not only that day but the next day, the first day of the week, when they would have begun the tradition of celebrating that day as 'the Lord's Day' (*Domenica* in Latin) or Sunday as we know it. Christians go to church on Sundays because it is the day on which Jesus rose, the day after the sabbath (Saturday).

Now presumably with Thomas among them, they are (to paraphrase Eliot) not there to verify, study or satisfy curiosity, but rather to kneel in a place where prayer has been authentically offered by many people over many years. Men and women, praying unceasingly together. It was radical and novel, countercultural and controversial. As we look back through time's glass doors at their fresh, lively prayerful faith, are we inspired to such authenticity? Or are we blasé about church life and liturgy? Yet, whether we think in terms of sabbath or the Lord's Day, it is never too late or too soon, nor too silly or old-fashioned, to kneel in prayer, together or alone.

Lord help me pray, today and every day. Amen

GORDON GILES

Lots of room

So one of the men who have accompanied us throughout the time that the Lord Jesus went in and out among us, beginning from the baptism of John until the day when he was taken up from us – one of these must become a witness with us to his resurrection.' So they proposed two, Joseph called Barsabbas, who was also known as Justus, and Matthias. Then they prayed and said, 'Lord, you know everyone's heart. Show us which one of these two you have chosen to take the place in this ministry and apostleship from which Judas turned aside to go to his own place.' And they cast lots for them, and the lot fell on Matthias; and he was added to the eleven apostles.

Mathematical probability is the basis on which so many people make decisions, for better or worse. All gambling is based on probability, whether completely random (as in a lottery) or with the extra dimension of 'form' (football pools and horse racing, with their favourites and outsiders).

Some people use probability to determine their faith. Yet belief is not about probability: God either raised Christ from the dead, or did not. This is the problem with probability: it sets out to *predict* the likelihood of things, not *determine* whether they happened. An event such as the resurrection did not 'not happen' because it was unlikely.

Many say we should not gamble with matters of faith. Yet the apostles, in seeking to decide between two favourites, draw lots (the equivalent of tossing a coin), expecting God to influence the result. Although there is lots of room in the disciples' team, they decided there had to be a substitute to join the first eleven. It was a culturally acceptable, pragmatic approach, and God made his will known through it.

Today we would not determine someone's vocation by tossing a coin, although where it is impossible to decide between two people seeking a particular role one might yet remember the difficult, divinely sanctioned decision that was made in that upper room.

---

*God, help me to never gamble with grace, but always find room
for your will in my heart. Amen*

GORDON GILES

Room for the Spirit

When the day of Pentecost had come, they were all together in one place. And suddenly from heaven there came a sound like the rush of a violent wind, and it filled the entire house where they were sitting. Divided tongues, as of fire, appeared among them, and a tongue rested on each of them. All of them were filled with the Holy Spirit and began to speak in other languages, as the Spirit gave them ability.

Tomorrow, Pentecost, is the day we celebrate God sending the Holy Spirit to be the comforter – the living breath of God in Jesus' disciples – 50 days after Easter, and daily since. Many believe it took place in the same upper room we have occupied this week. There is a nice roundness to the idea, although we can see above that the text does not specify that it was the same room. It is, however, a fair assumption, because Luke mentions 'the room upstairs where they were staying' (Acts 1:13). Since the word 'Pentecost' is derived from the Greek word for the 50th day after Passover, we know that the upper room was their headquarters for those seven weeks, which the church has developed into a seven-week Eastertide season. Thus it is just over seven weeks ago in the same upper room that Jesus was among them offering Passover bread and wine as his body and blood; and four days later he appeared to them on Easter Day.

Notwithstanding our focus on that place and period, the purpose of Pentecost is to relocate faith away from specific places for worship and reverence and carry faith into the spiritual spaces in our own hearts and minds, where we can make real room for God. Pentecost was the beginning of an outward movement, as the disciples began to spread abroad the good news of the saving death and resurrection of Jesus. Pentecost is about the Spirit dwelling everywhere, not just in one place or city. For seven weeks the disciples shut themselves away in a room above street level, hiding from the Roman and religious authorities. Yet whatever happened in that upper room turned their inward-looking fear into outgoing, missionary, courageous faith.

Open our doors, Jesus, that there may be room for faith everywhere. Amen

GORDON GILES

The sermon on the mount: Matthew 5—7

What is the scriptural core of our faith and life as Christians? Some might say Romans 8, or some other part of the epistles. Some might say the gospel accounts of Jesus' death or his resurrection. Anabaptists/Mennonites like myself are likely to say the sermon on the mount. The reason for this is summed up in a saying by one of the founders of the Anabaptist movement in the 16th century: 'No one can truly know Christ unless they follow him in life' (Hans Denck, 1495–1527). The epistle writer John said much the same:

Now by this we may be sure that we know him, if we obey his commandments. Whoever says, 'I have come to know him', but does not obey his commandments, is a liar, and in such a person the truth does not exist; but whoever obeys his word, truly in this person the love of God has reached perfection. By this we may be sure that we are in him: whoever says, 'I abide in him', ought to walk just as he walked.

1 JOHN 2:3–6 (NRSV)

I have heard it taught that the sermon on the mount is only there to make us aware of our own sin, to show us how unable we are to follow Jesus' ways. To say this is surely to distort Jesus' words – nothing in the sermon itself implies this. Jesus teaches in such a way that he clearly expects his disciples to obey his teaching. He outlines a way of life that is humble, compassionate, risk-taking and self-denying for the sake of others.

Of course, without the energy given by God's Spirit and by working with fellow disciples, we cannot achieve this. It is a corporate endeavour, not an individual one – 'Just as the branch cannot bear fruit by itself unless it abides in the vine, neither can you unless you abide in me' (John 15:4). The way of love is costly and demanding, and no one can walk it alone.

Many a sermon challenges, but perhaps few inspire or encourage (I say this as a preacher!). Jesus' extended sermon does both. As we study it, may we be inspired and strengthened to join our fellow believers in walking as Jesus walked, not just talking as he talked.

VERONICA ZUNDEL

Down is up

When Jesus saw the crowds, he went up the mountain; and after he sat down, his disciples came to him. Then he began to speak, and taught them, saying: 'Blessed are the poor in spirit, for theirs is the kingdom of heaven. Blessed are those who mourn, for they will be comforted. Blessed are the meek, for they will inherit the earth. Blessed are those who hunger and thirst for righteousness, for they will be filled.'

Here is something I have never noticed before: Jesus has not gone up the mountain to be heard by 'the crowds', as depicted in many illustrations. Rather, he goes to get away from the crowds and to give teaching to those who are already his disciples. This is not general wisdom for the world; it is guidance for those who have already chosen to follow him.

Unlike the ten commandments, the beatitudes (or blessings) are not commands at all. As the late Mennonite teacher Alan Kreider said, they are descriptive, not prescriptive. Jesus is not telling his followers to be poor in spirit (humble, vulnerable) or to mourn or to be meek or to yearn for justice in the world. He is describing people who are already like that, and calling them 'blessed' or happy.

It is hard, through our familiarity with it, to grasp how shocking this teaching would have been. In the disciples' thinking (and sometimes in ours), anyone who was rich, who had high status, who had no dissatisfaction with the world, was blessed by God and had clearly done something right. Jesus teaches the exact opposite. The lowly, the marginalised, those who live with bereavement or injustice, are the truly blessed. In their mindset of punishment and reward, the disciples would have thought such people cursed by God, having done something wrong. Jesus is reversing all the world's values.

Furthermore, in Luke's version of this 'sermon', Jesus pronounces curses on the rich, the well-fed and those who laugh at their good fortune (Luke 6:24–25). Instead it is the deprived, the grieving and those who long for justice who are closest to God and will meet God in their suffering.

Does your church honour those who are struggling, overlooked and sad, or does it accuse them of having little faith?

VERONICA ZUNDEL

Life in the kingdom

'Blessed are the merciful, for they will receive mercy. Blessed are the pure in heart, for they will see God. Blessed are the peacemakers, for they will be called children of God. Blessed are those who are persecuted for righteousness' sake, for theirs is the kingdom of heaven. Blessed are you when people revile you and persecute you and utter all kinds of evil against you falsely on my account. Rejoice and be glad, for your reward is great in heaven, for in the same way they persecuted the prophets who were before you.'

One way in which the beatitudes do echo the ten commandments is that the first half is more about attitudes and the second half more about behaviour towards others. Disciples of Jesus are meant to show mercy and compassion, not judgement. We are to be single-minded in our pursuit of God's kingdom. We are to make peace among our sisters and brothers, not to stir up division. And when we are criticised or attacked for our actions, we are to not only accept it but even rejoice in it, for criticism is a common experience for those who speak the truth.

However, we should not conclude that if people are against us, we must be right. Sometimes it may be our narrowness, our judgmentalism, that gets us into trouble. We need to be sure that any unpopularity stems from our compassion, our attempts to make peace or our calls for justice. When we try to be a bridge between opposing groups, we are likely to get walked over.

These blessings are not rules, nor a summary of 'the Christian way' to do anything and everything. They are an outline of what sort of people true disciples are. We become these people not by frantic effort and comprehensive rule-making, but simply by following Jesus, walking in step with his Spirit (2 Corinthians 3:5–6; Galatians 5:25).

People said of the early church (which still had its problems, being composed of humans): 'See how these Christians love one another.' Love, not perfection, is the mark of a true disciple.

'Let love be genuine; hate what is evil, hold fast to what is good;
love one another with mutual affection; outdo one another
in showing honour' (Romans 12:9–10).

VERONICA ZUNDEL

This little light of mine

'You are the salt of the earth; but if salt has lost its taste, how can its saltiness be restored? It is no longer good for anything, but is thrown out and trampled under foot. You are the light of the world. A city built on a hill cannot be hidden. No one after lighting a lamp puts it under the bushel basket, but on the lampstand, and it gives light to all in the house. In the same way, let your light shine before others, so that they may see your good works and give glory to your Father in heaven.'

Christian interpreters have often majored on the preserving quality of salt in this reference. Christians, in this view, are the ones who conserve the traditional ways. This could not be further from Jesus' meaning. True, in the days before refrigeration, salt was useful for preserving food over the winter. But here Jesus focuses on the saltiness, the taste of salt: his followers are supposed to make the world tastier, to bring out its true flavour. We should not be known as the ones who make everything dull!

Another interpretation is also possible. Salt was used as a fertiliser in Jesus' time. As well as adding taste to life, we are to foster growth and fertility – to bring out others' potential, to foster growth so that there can be a harvest. We are not in the business of shutting the world, or people, down, but in the business of growing God's kingdom.

As for being light, the instruction to 'let your light shine' may appear to contradict things said later in the sermon on the mount about not displaying our righteousness. But I suspect letting light shine is different from waving it about and shouting how virtuous we are. Light shows what has been hidden in darkness; it enables us to see things as they truly are and to do what needs to be done. It is mind-boggling, really, to think that not only is Jesus the world's light, but that we his followers are, too, if we walk in his ways.

Recently, I went to a 'candlelit' concert – except that there were no candles! The whole purpose of light is to shine, not to be concealed.

VERONICA ZUNDEL

Enemy love

'But I say to you that if you are angry with a brother or sister, you will be liable to judgement; and if you insult a brother or sister, you will be liable to the council; and if you say, "You fool", you will be liable to the hell of fire. So when you are offering your gift at the altar, if you remember that your brother or sister has something against you, leave your gift there before the altar and go; first be reconciled to your brother or sister, and then come and offer your gift.'

There is a reason most churches share the peace before taking Communion together. Jesus teaches that our worship of God is meaningless unless we are reconciled with our brothers and sisters. But how many of us, during the sharing of the peace, approach anyone with whom we have been in conflict and at least make an appointment to talk things over? I suspect most of us greet the people we get on well with and somehow do not manage to get round to the rest of the church, including our 'enemies'.

You may think it strange of me to assume we will have enemies within the household of faith, but often it is those closest to us whom we find most difficult to get on with. In my Mennonite church, there was one person I found really hard to cope with. Then her husband became seriously ill, and I prayed for them both daily. I hope it made a difference, but I wish I had been reconciled to her before the church closed down and while we were regularly sharing bread and wine.

Not long ago I had a new insight into the well-loved Psalm 23. I reread the line 'You prepare a table before me in the presence of my enemies' (v. 5) and wondered what if this was not a case of showing off to the enemies how blessed we are by God, but a chance to invite them to share the food God had given us.

Jesus said, 'You have heard… But I say…' (Matthew 5:21). How prepared are we to re-examine traditions and ask if God is saying something new to us?

VERONICA ZUNDEL

Respect and truth

'You have heard that it was said, "You shall not commit adultery." But I say to you that everyone who looks at a woman with lust has already committed adultery with her in his heart. If your right eye causes you to sin, tear it out and throw it away; it is better for you to lose one of your members than for your whole body to be thrown into hell… Again, you have heard that it was said to those of ancient times, "You shall not swear falsely, but carry out the vows you have made to the Lord." But I say to you, Do not swear at all… Let your word be "Yes, Yes" or "No, No"; anything more than this comes from the evil one.'

I am not convinced that Jesus is condemning every teenager (of any gender) who is consumed with desire for a schoolmate or a pop icon. Nor do I think he is saying that even thinking about a woman with desire makes you a sinner. That is the way to constant guilt, and to seeing the female sex as nothing but a temptation.

I do believe Jesus is mainly addressing what feminists call 'the male gaze' here. It might be a valid paraphrase to render this as 'Do not objectify a woman as solely there for your own pleasure.' Jesus, in effect, is saying, 'Regard women first of all as fellow human beings rather than as sexual objects.' He is also asking men to take responsibility for their own desires and fantasies and not to blame them on women. Of course, the same applies to women looking at men and to those whose desire is for the same gender. Other people are not there for our gratification.

As for the teaching on swearing, in context it clearly has nothing to do with uttering the odd four-letter word. It is about not making meaningless promises which you cannot keep. Mennonites and Quakers are among the Christian traditions who take this literally and refuse to swear the oath in court. This is because we expect ourselves to tell truth at all times, not just when under oath.

Lord, purify my attitudes as well as my actions. Let me be truthful and to treat others with respect.

VERONICA ZUNDEL

A new way

'You have heard that it was said, "An eye for an eye and a tooth for a tooth." But I say to you, Do not resist an evildoer. But if anyone strikes you on the right cheek, turn the other also… You have heard that it was said, "You shall love your neighbour and hate your enemy." But I say to you, Love your enemies and pray for those who persecute you, so that you may be children of your Father in heaven; for he makes his sun rise on the evil and on the good, and sends rain on the righteous and on the unrighteous. For if you love those who love you, what reward do you have? Do not even the tax-collectors do the same?'

I once gave a talk on Hebrews 1:1–2 – 'Long ago God spoke to our ancestors in many and various ways by the prophets, but in these last days he has spoken to us by a Son.' I focused on the 'but' in the middle, stressing the discontinuity of Jesus' revelation with that in the Old Testament, as well as its continuity. After the talk, someone more educated in New Testament Greek than I came and pointed out that the word 'but' is not actually in the Greek! Nevertheless, it is implied, and most translations use it.

In today's passage, Jesus' is teaching a new instruction: that we should not retaliate but love those who attack us. The Old Testament law was already an improvement on the unlimited vengeance that went before: it implies '*only* an eye for an eye, and *only* a tooth for a tooth'. But Jesus goes further. This is a hard lesson, and one that is never going to be easy to practise.

Some years ago there was a shooting in an Amish school in the USA. Teachers and pupils were killed, and the gunman then shot himself. The Amish community immediately announced that they forgave the shooter, and reached out to his widow and children. I do not know how they managed this, but I suspect it was the outcome of a lifetime of practice forgiving each other.

'Hurt people hurt people', goes the saying. Teach us, Lord,
to break the cycle of hurt.

VERONICA ZUNDEL

Against public piety

'So whenever you give alms, do not sound a trumpet before you, as the hypocrites do in the synagogues and in the streets, so that they may be praised by others. Truly I tell you, they have received their reward. But when you give alms, do not let your left hand know what your right hand is doing, so that your alms may be done in secret; and your Father who sees in secret will reward you. And whenever you pray, do not be like the hypocrites; for they love to stand and pray in the synagogues and at the street corners, so that they may be seen by others. Truly I tell you, they have received their reward. But whenever you pray, go into your room and shut the door and pray to your Father who is in secret; and your Father who sees in secret will reward you.'

I'm an enthusiast for Facebook, which my film-critic friend calls 'the water cooler for the self-employed' – where those of us who work alone can gather during the working day. However, I feel very ambivalent about people posting their prayers on Facebook – isn't this the modern equivalent of Jesus' contemporaries standing on street corners to say lengthy prayers?

Perhaps the key word in this passage is 'reward', a word that occurs repeatedly in the sermon on the mount. I went to a weekend retreat about suffering recently, where it was stressed that suffering is not a punishment for sin and, conversely, good fortune is not a reward for righteousness. Jesus uses the language of reward differently in his teaching. We are not to look for rewards for our good actions in this life: rewards such as people calling us philanthropists or seeing us as saintly. With some humour, he points out that those who seek such worldly recognition have already had their reward, and that is all they will get. But if we give and pray with no outward display and no expectation of recognition, there is an eternal reward for us: that God, not our neighbour, will be 'well pleased' (Matthew 3:17; 17:5).

'The kings of the Gentiles lord it over them; and those in authority over them are called benefactors. But not so with you' (Luke 22:25–26a).

VERONICA ZUNDEL

Praying with reality

'When you are praying, do not heap up empty phrases as the Gentiles do; for they think that they will be heard because of their many words. Do not be like them, for your Father knows what you need before you ask him. Pray then in this way: Our Father in heaven, hallowed be your name. Your kingdom come. Your will be done, on earth as it is in heaven. Give us this day our daily bread. And forgive us our debts, as we also have forgiven our debtors. And do not bring us to the time of trial, but rescue us from the evil one.'

The tradition of spontaneous prayer in small groups has much in its favour. It teaches us that prayers do not have to be eloquent, and gives us confidence in asking honestly for God's intervention. But it is also easily parodied for our tendency to use stock phrases ('We just really pray…') and Christian jargon. Sometimes a prewritten prayer helps us move beyond our own narrow perspectives.

I wonder what the 'empty phrases' uttered by the Gentiles really were. I wonder if it was a case of intoning and declaiming at great length, using fancy words, on the assumption that God was hard of hearing and needed to be harangued! Our prayers can so easily become dominated by anxiety rather than faith.

In contrast Jesus gives his disciples a short and simple prayer that covers all aspects of our life as believers: honouring God, desiring God's kingdom, crying out for God's will to prevail, asking for daily provision, seeking forgiveness and a merciful heart, and praying for protection from testing and suffering. We perhaps know this model of prayer a little too well. We pray it as a standard feature of our worship, hardly thinking about the words. It was only when praying it with thousands of others in a field at the Greenbelt Festival that I realised 'Your will be done' is not an act of resignation but a desperate cry for good to triumph in this sad, violent world. It is a prayer to pray with our whole heart, and even with our tears.

'In his anguish he prayed more earnestly, and his sweat became like great drops of blood falling down on the ground' (Luke 22:44).

VERONICA ZUNDEL

The safest investment

'Do not store up for yourselves treasures on earth, where moth and rust consume and where thieves break in and steal; but store up for yourselves treasures in heaven, where neither moth nor rust consumes and where thieves do not break in and steal. For where your treasure is, there your heart will be also. The eye is the lamp of the body. So, if your eye is healthy, your whole body will be full of light; but if your eye is unhealthy, your whole body will be full of darkness. If then the light in you is darkness, how great is the darkness! No one can serve two masters; for a slave will either hate the one and love the other, or be devoted to the one and despise the other. You cannot serve God and wealth.'

Jesus has a lot to say about money in the gospels. Perhaps this is because we are so prone to find our security in having enough to keep us from disaster. But as he points out here, money and possessions are vulnerable. Your investments may go down as well as up! I have had a cashmere jumper eaten by moths, and a burglary robbed me of jewellery I had inherited from my small extended family.

What does it mean, then, to accumulate treasure in heaven? It may mean creating a 'deposit' of kindness, generosity and goodness towards others – wealth which lasts forever and is not made by exploiting others. It may also mean learning to live on the edge, relying on God for our security rather than hiding under a blanket of financial protection.

It is interesting that this teaching on false and true wealth is intertwined with a parable about healthy or unhealthy eyes. The eye here stands for our perception of the world. Think of those animations where a character suddenly has dollar signs appear in his eyes – a prime example of the unhealthy eye! Rather, our vision should be clear of greed, seeing the world as God's gift and believing that as God's children, our destiny is safe – even if we may have to go through times of deprivation or vulnerability.

When did your church last have a talk about money that wasn't an appeal for funds?

VERONICA ZUNDEL

Don't worry, be happy

'Therefore I tell you, do not worry about your life, what you will eat or what you will drink, or about your body, what you will wear... Look at the birds of the air; they neither sow nor reap nor gather into barns, and yet your heavenly Father feeds them. Are you not of more value than they? And can any of you by worrying add a single hour to your span of life? And why do you worry about clothing? Consider the lilies of the field, how they grow; they neither toil nor spin, yet I tell you, even Solomon in all his glory was not clothed like one of these. But if God so clothes the grass of the field, which is alive today and tomorrow is thrown into the oven, will he not much more clothe you – you of little faith?... But strive first for the kingdom of God and his righteousness, and all these things will be given to you as well.'

When my son tells me off for worrying about him, I say, 'It's my job.' I grew up with a model of parenting where anxiety equalled love. Given my parents were Holocaust refugees, it is hardly surprising.

As Jesus points out clearly here, worry achieves nothing, except to make others anxious too. If we have faith in God's love, we should believe in God's provision too. We might say that God does not appear to provide for those living in war-torn or drought-ridden countries. But is it God's job to provide for them – or is it ours, through giving to aid agencies and lobbying our government for more help? If we gave less energy (and money) to trying to provide for ourselves, would we have more to spare to help others who are more needy?

I suspect there are also anxious versions of Christian faith, where we preach forgiveness and yet live with anxiety that we might inadvertently fall into sin. This is another reason to consider the birds and flowers, who simply get on with living life as best they can. For humans, our focus should be on working for the rule of God in the world, not for our own security or even purity.

Lord, teach me what it means to prioritise your kingdom.

VERONICA ZUNDEL

Sitting in judgement

'Do not judge, so that you may not be judged. For with the judgement you make you will be judged, and the measure you give will be the measure you get. Why do you see the speck in your neighbour's eye, but do not notice the log in your own eye? Or how can you say to your neighbour, "Let me take the speck out of your eye", while the log is in your own eye? You hypocrite, first take the log out of your own eye, and then you will see clearly to take the speck out of your neighbour's eye.'

There is an old Jewish joke which goes: the rabbi prostrated himself before the sanctuary and cried, 'Lord, have mercy on me, a mere worm.' Then the cantor did likewise. Finally, the caretaker knelt and cried, 'Lord, have mercy on me, a mere worm.' The cantor turned to the rabbi and said, 'Look who thinks he's a worm now!'

We live in an age of judgementalism: on social media, in the news and in magazines and newspapers. We are always being called either to make judgments on how others live, look and speak or to compare ourselves unfavourably with others who appear to be doing better (even though we know the photos of them have been manipulated and the interviews or profiles are selective).

Jesus' contemporaries did not have social media, so there was less self-judgement or impostor syndrome, and he focused on our tendency to condemn others. One's confidence in one's own righteousness is always enhanced by comparing it to others' sins! If yesterday's reading was about trusting God to provide for our own needs, today's is about trusting God to deal with others' faults and letting go of the right to point them out ourselves.

I have observed a style of preaching where the idea of 'application' of the Bible seems to be boiled down to 'Do more of X, do less of Y.' This is a recipe for spreading guilt and inadequacy. How about we major instead on encouragement, inspiration and training in goodness?

'When they kept on questioning him, he... said to them, "Let anyone among you who is without sin be the first to throw a stone at her"' (John 8:7).

VERONICA ZUNDEL

Never be afraid to ask

'Ask, and it will be given you; search, and you will find; knock, and the door will be opened for you. For everyone who asks receives, and everyone who searches finds, and for everyone who knocks, the door will be opened. Is there anyone among you who, if your child asks for bread, will give a stone? Or if the child asks for a fish, will give a snake? If you then, who are evil, know how to give good gifts to your children, how much more will your Father in heaven give good things to those who ask him!'

My late mother-in-law was asked by a grandchild, 'Can you get me an ice cream, Nana?' She replied, 'That'll be the last thing I do.' At the end of the outing, the child said, 'So now will you buy me an ice cream?' Children are both very literal and very trusting!

Ten years ago I wrote a book called *Everything I Know about God, I've Learned from Being a Parent* (BRF, 2013). It charted my experience of parenting a child with special needs and the insights it gave me into God's parenting of us. When I finished the book, I realised the whole thing had been an extended meditation on these verses.

A good parent will not meet requests with denial. But note that Jesus promises only that God will give 'good things', not necessarily anything we fancy. A good parent may not always give precisely what the child wants, like the story of the 'little alien' I read about in a parenting book who wanted a chainsaw for Christmas! Still, essentially God is a giver, not a denier. God would always rather say 'Yes' than 'No', unless 'No' is the kinder, wiser answer. And often God may say, 'Wait.'

What if our prayers seem to be unanswered for years? Jesus encourages us to keep asking, seeking, knocking, without giving up. Above all, he asks us to hold on to our image of God as good and to never conclude that God is against us.

'And will not God grant justice to his chosen ones who cry to him day and night? Will he delay long in helping them? I tell you, he will quickly grant justice to them' (Luke 18:7–8a).

VERONICA ZUNDEL

The fruit test

'In everything do to others as you would have them do to you; for this is the law and the prophets… Beware of false prophets, who come to you in sheep's clothing but inwardly are ravenous wolves. You will know them by their fruits… Not everyone who says to me, "Lord, Lord," will enter the kingdom of heaven, but only one who does the will of my Father in heaven. On that day many will say to me, "Lord, Lord, did we not prophesy in your name, and cast out demons in your name, and do many deeds of power in your name?" Then I will declare to them, "I never knew you; go away from me, you evildoers."

As I write this, several prominent church leaders in the USA have had to step down because of alleged or confessed sexual misconduct. They converted or encouraged many, they developed groundbreaking ministries, yet they could not manage to practise basic self-control. Just because we do spectacular things in Jesus' name does not mean we are his disciples.

This is scary teaching, especially for Christian leaders. An 'effective' ministry does not mean we are actually doing God's will. It is possible to bandy Jesus' name about and yet not follow him. Perhaps the bigger we get in our own estimation and our public role, the harder it is to fit through that narrow gate Jesus asks us to enter through (Matthew 7:13–14)! The broad way is so much easier.

This is one area where Jesus does ask us to judge others – to assess, but not to condemn. A tree cannot weigh its own fruit, but those who come to harvest the fruit can. We can assess the quality of leaders' discipleship by its outcomes: does their work produce true disciples or create unhealthy dependency and cult-like adulation? Those who most desire leadership are not necessarily the best ones to have it.

The Amish select elders by lot. In an old story, an Amish man is listed but does not get selected. When asked how he feels, he answers, 'Like I got shot at and missed!'

'The greatest among you must become like the youngest, and the leader like one who serves… I am among you as one who serves' (Luke 22:26–27).

VERONICA ZUNDEL

Bedrock

'Everyone then who hears these words of mine and acts on them will be like a wise man who built his house on rock. The rain fell, the floods came, and the winds blew and beat on that house, but it did not fall, because it had been founded on rock. And everyone who hears these words of mine and does not act on them will be like a foolish man who built his house on sand. The rain fell, and the floods came, and the winds blew and beat against that house, and it fell – and great was its fall!' Now when Jesus had finished saying these things, the crowds were astounded at his teaching, for he taught them as one having authority, and not as their scribes.

In San Francisco, the 58-storey Millennium Tower, constructed in 2009, is both sinking and tilting. The reason, according to critics, is that the reinforced concrete piles on which it stands only extend into the soft clay beneath, not right down to the bedrock. It is a matter of foundations.

Note that Jesus does not say the 'rock' on which we should be founded is 'sound' doctrine. Rather, it is whether we hear his words and act on them. Orthodoxy – right doctrine – is important, but not so much as orthopraxis – right living. In his book *Saving God from Religion* (Penguin Random House, 2020), Robin R. Meyers writes: 'In the Sermon on the Mount, there is not a single word about what to believe, only words about what to do and what to be. By the time the Nicene Creed is written, only three centuries later, there is not a single word in it about what to do and how to be – only words about what to believe.'

It is following Jesus' ways, not invoking his name or believing certain things about him, that is the bedrock which will save us from sinking. That is the whole point of the sermon on the mount. This is not 'salvation by works', but it is salvation *for* works.

'For if while we were enemies, we were reconciled to God through the death of his Son, much more surely, having been reconciled, will we be saved by his life' (Romans 5:10).

VERONICA ZUNDEL

Mark 7—10

By the time we reach chapter 7 of his gospel, we find Mark well into his stride. His style is to give the good news to us straight, and usually with some urgency. 'Immediately' is a word that regularly crops up in his gospel. Thus, Jesus, after his dramatic baptism by John, is thrust into the wilderness for his time of testing, and then comes back proclaiming the gospel of the kingdom of heaven, assembling his team of followers and getting down to business. And that business includes miracles of every kind: deliverance from evil; healings of all manner of sickness; raising a girl from death; calming a storm; feeding thousands of people with a few fish and loaves; and walking on water. In addition Jesus regularly preaches to the multitudes, telling stories based on scenes from everyday life. It is clear he is a down-to-earth Messiah releasing the wisdom, energy and grace of heaven to the mortals he so clearly loves.

There is no slackening of the pace from chapter 7 onwards, but we do start to get hints of the dark clouds that are to come. Chapter 10 marks the end of those wonderful years when he and his team of disciples freely roamed the land proclaiming the kingdom and demonstrating it with extraordinary wonders. After Mark 11 the scene moves to Jerusalem, where the action slows and the shadow of the cross falls across the narrative.

In the next couple of weeks we shall join Mark's story with the momentum of the early chapters which have brought us this far. We are taken into further stories of liberating encounters with struggling and suffering humanity. Yet we are also aware of the growing menace of the religious authorities. There are also disturbances in the disciple camp. And three of these disciples witness the utterly astonishing spectacle of Jesus being transfigured in a cloud of glory. We come to these chapters as adventurers and explorers. The stories may be very familiar to us, but it is the curious power of all scripture that frequently even the best-known passages contain a few surprises that can lead us to new discoveries which both delight and disturb us.

MICHAEL MITTON

The perils of lip service

Now when the Pharisees and some of the scribes who had come from Jerusalem gathered around him, they noticed that some of his disciples were eating with defiled hands, that is, without washing them... So the Pharisees and the scribes asked him, 'Why do your disciples not live according to the tradition of the elders, but eat with defiled hands?' He said to them, 'Isaiah prophesied rightly about you hypocrites, as it is written, "This people honours me with their lips, but their hearts are far from me."'

The religious culture in which Jesus lived was one of fastidious law-keeping. God was seen as a deity easily offended. You had to work very hard to keep on the right side of him. This was achieved by observing the law as defined in the first five books of the Bible. In the fourth and fifth centuries before Christ, there developed a group of legal experts called the scribes. They were passionate about detail regarding how you carried out your observance of the law. Thus there were precise rules about how to wash your hands before eating, thereby making yourself ritually clean before your meal. The primary concern of the Pharisees and scribes was not hygiene, but ritual purity. How could Jesus possibly claim to be an authoritative teacher if his disciples were so blatantly disregarding a set of rules that all God-fearing people were obliged to follow?

As Jesus so often does, he answers one question with another, and it is his question which goes straight to the heart of the matter. Jesus can see that this obsession with observing the details of the law has produced a religion of lip service, and that kind of service has only succeeded in driving the hearts of the people away from God. In fact, he goes as far as saying that their obsession with human traditions causes them to break the very commandments that they are so intent on keeping (see Mark 7:8). Jesus saw that a religion that imposed rigorous law-keeping on people only alienated them from the God they were trying to serve. His way was to empower people to open their hearts in love to God.

What draws your heart closer to God?

MICHAEL MITTON

Truly clean

From there he set out and went away to the region of Tyre… A woman whose little daughter had an unclean spirit immediately heard about him, and she came and bowed down at his feet. Now the woman was a Gentile, of Syrophoenician origin. She begged him to cast the demon out of her daughter. He said to her, 'Let the children be fed first, for it is not fair to take the children's food and throw it to the dogs.' But she answered him, 'Sir, even the dogs under the table eat the children's crumbs.' Then he said to her, 'For saying that, you may go – the demon has left your daughter.'

The coastal Gentile city of Tyre lay 40 miles north-west of Capernaum. Jesus and his friends would have been impressed by both its famous harbour, with ships from many nations, and its strong fortress. It was an independent city with its own king, gods and coinage. This is a very different world to that of our last story, which ended with Jesus teaching about his understanding of what is clean and unclean (see 7:1–23). Here in Tyre, he is now immersed in a Gentile world that the scribes and Pharisees would regard as distinctly unclean.

Then, a Gentile woman arrives asking for help for her daughter with an unclean spirit: even more ritual uncleanness. Jesus responds with apparent rudeness, effectively declaring her no better than a dog. 'Dog' was a common word of contempt for a Gentile, but Jesus does not use the usual word that referred to wild street dogs, but rather the one used for the dogs that were pets and highly regarded. He is adjusting the normal use of the word. Perhaps the woman recognised this, knowing that children love their pet dogs.

The religious world of the time aimed to evaluate people according to religious qualifications. But Jesus was demonstrating a new order of no such distinctions, and this Gentile woman seems to have grasped this. As a result, the unclean spirit departs. Thus the woman knows that Jesus regards her as clean.

Do we still evaluate people according to religious qualifications?

MICHAEL MITTON

The empathetic ephphatha

Then he returned from the region of Tyre, and went by way of Sidon towards the Sea of Galilee, in the region of the Decapolis. They brought to him a deaf man who had an impediment in his speech; and they begged him to lay his hand on him. He took him aside in private, away from the crowd, and put his fingers into his ears, and he spat and touched his tongue. Then looking up to heaven, he sighed and said to him, 'Ephphatha', that is, 'Be opened.' And immediately his ears were opened, his tongue was released, and he spoke plainly.

This story reveals a high degree of sensitivity by Jesus to the man who is hearing-impaired and has a speech impediment. The friends who bring him want Jesus to lay hands straight away on the man. But Jesus senses that the man has little clue what the laying on of hands would mean. So he takes him to a quiet and private place where the man will not be distracted by extraneous activity. Jesus puts his fingers into the man's ears, thereby making it very clear that he is attending to his hearing difficulty. He then spits, for in that world, spittle was regarded as having curative qualities. This action, therefore, along with the touching of his tongue, tells the man that Jesus is now attending to his speech problem.

Then Jesus looks upward, and the man would have recognised this as an appeal to heaven for help. He says 'Ephphatha', which, I am told, is a word that can be readily understood by those who listen through sign language. The word means 'be opened', and at its uttering the man's hearing returns and he is able to speak freely.

If the story of the woman in Tyre speaks of Jesus being willing to dwell in her 'unclean' world, this story speaks of Jesus' willingness to dwell in an 'unhealed' world. His incarnation involved dwelling close to all conditions of humanity. For those struggling with any kind of sickness or disability, this is a comforting story, for it tells us that Jesus has a high sensitivity to whatever world we may find ourselves inhabiting.

Thank you, Lord Jesus, that you dwell close to me, whatever my situation in life. Amen

MICHAEL MITTON

Beyond the superficial

Now the disciples had forgotten to bring any bread; and they had only one loaf with them in the boat. And he cautioned them, saying, 'Watch out – beware of the yeast of the Pharisees and the yeast of Herod.' They said to one another, 'It is because we have no bread.' And becoming aware of it, Jesus said to them, 'Why are you talking about having no bread? Do you still not perceive or understand? Are your hearts hardened? Do you have eyes, and fail to see? Do you have ears, and fail to hear? And do you not remember?'

This passage comes directly after the miraculous multiplication of bread and fish. It is the second such miracle recorded by Mark (see 6:30–44). There is therefore something humorous about the disciples worrying about having a lack of bread. Had they not seen how Jesus could multiply bread?

Jesus uses the opportunity to speak about the yeast of the Pharisees and Herod. We normally think of yeast as a good component of bread-making, but here Jesus is clearly thinking of it as a corrupting influence. He has observed how some of the religious authorities have introduced an oppressive ingredient into the religion that has terribly damaged it.

He then turns to his disciples in the boat and questions them hard. They are worried about not having enough bread, and his response is to get them to question the quality of their hearts, their eyes and their ears. Jesus frequently urges them to see beyond the immediate and to learn through a sensitised heart, and through perception and deep listening. This discipline includes a faith-inducing remembering. Remember, says Jesus, those miraculous feedings. What does this tell you about your Father in heaven? The Pharisees are so focused on the outward and therefore live superficially. But if the disciples can develop a perceptive heart, they will develop kingdom-of-God instincts.

Jesus uses every opportunity to call the disciples to use all kinds of life experiences, even a rumbling tummy, to develop faith muscles. The discipline is simple: go beyond the superficial by pausing, feeling, listening, seeing and remembering.

How might God lead you to pause, feel, listen, see and remember today?

MICHAEL MITTON

Seeing things

They came to Bethsaida. Some people brought a blind man to him and begged him to touch him. He took the blind man by the hand and led him out of the village; and when he had put saliva on his eyes and laid his hands on him, he asked him, 'Can you see anything?' And the man looked up and said, 'I can see people, but they look like trees, walking.' Then Jesus laid his hands on his eyes again; and he looked intently and his sight was restored, and he saw everything clearly.

Mark places this healing story right after the discussion about yeast that we considered yesterday. That story was about learning to perceive beyond the outer impression. Today's story is about a literal restoration of sight. Jesus is back by the Sea of Galilee, and some people come to him with a friend who is blind. They beg Jesus to heal him.

We then have a very touching scene of Jesus taking the man by the hand and leading him out of the village. As with the deaf man (7:31–35), Jesus treats this man with great sensitivity. Again he uses saliva to indicate a healing action. This is the only healing story to happen in stages. The man appears at first to be only half-healed. There are a few people around, and the man, as he receives his sight, views them as like walking trees. It is a precious insight into what it must be like for a blind person to start seeing again. Jesus then completes the healing and the man sees perfectly.

Among other things, this is another story that tells us the personal and sensitive approach of Jesus' healing ministry. He is no healer ranting from a stage, distant from the people. He walks hand in hand with them. The gradualness of this literal healing may have a reference to the previous kind of spiritual seeing. It may be telling us that insight and perception do not have to happen instantly. As we begin to 'see', we may find it hard to understand. But let Jesus keep working on us, and in time we will see clearly.

Lord Jesus, lead me away from my busy world and open my eyes to your wonders. Amen

MICHAEL MITTON

Who am I?

Jesus went on with his disciples to the villages of Caesarea Philippi; and on the way he asked his disciples, 'Who do people say that I am?' And they answered him, 'John the Baptist; and others, Elijah; and still others, one of the prophets.' He asked them, 'But who do you say that I am?' Peter answered him, 'You are the Messiah.' And he sternly ordered them not to tell anyone about him.

We have reached the middle of Mark's gospel, and it is a pivotal point. We often think of this story as the testing of the disciples' faith in Jesus. But it is also a test of Jesus' faith in the disciples. Had he taught them enough for them to fully believe that he was the Messiah? Would their faith be strong enough to tread the tough road ahead of them?

Jesus asks his disciples this question about his identity in an interesting place. Caesarea Philippi was outside Galilee. It had once been the centre of Baal worship and was also believed to be the birthplace of the Greek god Pan. In this town there stood a prominent temple built as a place to worship Caesar as a god. So it is a place that is highly charged with ancient and modern religions and the worship of Roman power. And it is here that this humble craftsman from Galilee asks his friends who they think he is.

Surely to Jesus' delight and relief, Peter answers confidently that he believes Jesus to be the Messiah. You would think, once he has seen that his disciples know who he is, Jesus would tell them to spread the message abroad. But no, they are to tell nobody because they do not yet know what this means. They have their ideas about the glorious Messiah, but Jesus needs to teach them about the road of suffering that is part of the Messiah story.

From time to time, it is good to imagine that Jesus comes to us in our world of many gods and political and economic powers, and asks us the same question. Can he rely on us to believe him, and walk his road of both glory and suffering?

'Who do you say that I am?'

MICHAEL MITTON

Recognising the Messiah

Then he began to teach them that the Son of Man must undergo great suffering, and be rejected by the elders, the chief priests, and the scribes, and be killed, and after three days rise again. He said all this quite openly. And Peter took him aside and began to rebuke him. But turning and looking at his disciples, he rebuked Peter and said, 'Get behind me, Satan! For you are setting your mind not on divine things but on human things.' He called the crowd with his disciples, and said to them, 'If any want to become my followers, let them deny themselves and take up their cross and follow me.'

The disciples are on a high as they acknowledge that they are actually friends of the much longed-for Messiah. Since their earliest days, they have been taught about this coming Saviour. However, the messianic ideas of the time were nationalistic, violent and vengeful. The Messiah was seen as a powerful warrior, who would defeat his enemies and bring victory to the people of God. Yet the craftsman rabbi they have been following looks nothing like this, which makes it even more impressive that Peter should call Jesus the Messiah. But now, Jesus has to work to divest the disciples of their previous notions of the Messiah. Furthermore, he alarms them by telling them that he will suffer and be killed.

The disciples would never have seen vulnerability as part of the messianic message. So Peter rebukes Jesus and receives an even greater reprimand in return. He sees that behind Peter's understandable protection of Jesus is an insidious attack by Satan, who seeks to divert Jesus from the cross. Once again, Jesus is training his disciples to shift their minds from earthly instincts to a heavenly one. The earthly instinct will do its best to avoid all suffering. But the heavenly instinct has such confidence in God that it knows that if the path does involve suffering, resurrection will never be far away. Taking up the humility of the cross also involves taking up the glory of resurrection.

O Christ, when I must take up the sorrow of the cross, remind me
of the hope of resurrection life. Amen

MICHAEL MITTON

Seen in a new light

Six days later, Jesus took with him Peter and James and John, and led them up a high mountain apart, by themselves. And he was transfigured before them, and his clothes became dazzling white, such as no one on earth could bleach them. And there appeared to them Elijah with Moses, who were talking with Jesus... Then a cloud overshadowed them, and from the cloud there came a voice, 'This is my Son, the Beloved; listen to him!'

Jesus' teaching that he would have to suffer greatly was understandably a cause of huge disturbance among the disciples. But just as they are coming to terms with a Messiah who has to suffer, they are given a vision of extraordinary glory.

As Jesus took them up the mountain, they presumably felt he was leading them to a quiet retreat for some more teaching. The disturbing conversation about the cross six days earlier would still be ringing in their ears. Mark reports that at some point on this mountain retreat, Jesus' appearance changes dramatically. The simple robes of this hitherto normal-looking rabbi become so bright that no one can look at them. Then two of the great characters from the Old Testament arrive – the two who represent the law and the prophets. Somehow, Peter seems to know who they are. None of the disciples can disguise their terror at the brilliant spectacle, along with the unnerving manifestation of two men from history turning up on this hillside.

Then a mist rises and no doubt the disciples recognise this as the kind of cloud of glory in which Moses met with God on the mountain. And from this cloud comes the voice of God, which, with beautiful simplicity, declares God's love for his son. It is a voice addressed to the disciples, who are told to take note of all that the Son says. It is nothing complicated. It is to do with loving and listening.

The disciples could never be the same after this. They had literally seen Jesus in a new light, and no dark that awaited them could rob them of this light.

Lord Jesus, when the days are dark, open my eyes to see you as the Lord of glory. Amen

MICHAEL MITTON

Help my unbelief

They brought the boy to him. When the spirit saw him, immediately it threw the boy into convulsions, and he fell on the ground and rolled about, foaming at the mouth. Jesus asked the father, 'How long has this been happening to him?' And he said, 'From childhood. It has often cast him into the fire and into the water, to destroy him; but if you are able to do anything, have pity on us and help us.' Jesus said to him, 'If you are able! – All things can be done for the one who believes.' Immediately the father of the child cried out, 'I believe; help my unbelief!'

This central part of Mark's gospel is like riding a big dipper: we are up one minute and down the next. No sooner has the glorious cloud dispersed than the disciples walk down the hill with Jesus, who lowers the tone by once again talking about death (vv. 9–13). And then, depressingly, they find themselves back with a large crowd of people who are arguing with the religious teachers. What is more, there is a group of disconsolate disciples who have failed to rid a lad of his demons, and everyone is complaining. This is a long way from the glory of the mountaintop! Even Jesus shows a little exasperation at this (v. 19).

However, within this arguing and disgruntled crowd emerges the father of the lad and in him Jesus sees an encouraging flicker of light. This man, who is caught up in the general dark mood of the crowd, pleads to Jesus to have pity on his son. The mood in the camp seems to feel that Jesus is not up to this. Jesus changes the mood by looking for faith. What kind of faith does the man have? With commendable honesty, he confesses a mix of belief and unbelief. That appears to be enough for Jesus, for he then delivers the boy of his spirit, and all is well.

The valleys of our life journey can be tough, where we may carry a mix of belief and unbelief. But it is encouraging to read that all Jesus requires is our honesty. He does indeed help our unbelief.

Lord, today I believe. But please help my unbelief. Amen

MICHAEL MITTON

The Christ child

He asked them, 'What were you arguing about on the way?' But they were silent, for on the way they had argued with one another about who was the greatest. He sat down, called the twelve, and said to them, 'Whoever wants to be first must be last of all and servant of all.' Then he took a little child and put it among them; and taking it in his arms, he said to them, 'Whoever welcomes one such child in my name welcomes me, and whoever welcomes me welcomes not me but the one who sent me.'

On the way home from the mountain and the valley, Jesus speaks of his coming death and resurrection again, but the disciples find such talk difficult and alarming and dare not ask Jesus for more details (vv. 30–32). This anxiety does not bring out the best in them, for it provokes an argument about greatness. Was it that Peter, James and John were asserting some greatness from having seen the transfiguration? These disciples are so wonderfully human! They had hoped that this argument would not be overheard by Jesus, and they must have felt embarrassed to discover he had listened-in. Yet he does not rebuke them. Instead, with the shadow of the cross falling over the gospel now, Jesus uses this opportunity to teach about what greatness means for those who take on the culture of heaven.

They are in a house where there are children present. There is a touching warmth in this story as Jesus enfolds the child in his arms (as the literal translation of the Greek text puts it). Children in that culture had no power, rights or status of any kind. In any event, such things were not important: all that mattered was whether they were protected and loved. Jesus has had his own recent experience of his Father enfolding him in a cloud and expressing his love. So he says that by welcoming this child, you welcome him. In other words, Jesus is identifying with this child, and claiming no power or status other than being beloved. And almighty God's attitude is just the same. Heaven's idea of greatness is radically different to the world's.

How does Jesus' idea of greatness affect how you live today?

MICHAEL MITTON

The soft heart

Some Pharisees came, and to test him they asked, 'Is it lawful for a man to divorce his wife?' He answered them, 'What did Moses command you?' They said, 'Moses allowed a man to write a certificate of dismissal and to divorce her.' But Jesus said to them, 'Because of your hardness of heart he wrote this commandment for you. But from the beginning of creation, "God made them male and female." "For this reason a man shall leave his father and mother and be joined to his wife, and the two shall become one flesh." So they are no longer two, but one flesh. Therefore what God has joined together, let no one separate.'

As Jesus progresses towards Jerusalem, again he meets some Pharisees who are keen to catch him out and find some charge they can lay against him. They test him with a topical question. Jesus was in King Herod's area of jurisdiction, and only recently had John the Baptist chastised Herod for abandoning his wife for another woman.

Jesus replies to their question with a question of his own, which takes the discussion to a deeper level: what did Moses command? Sure enough, there is provision for divorce in Deuteronomy 24. This was convenient for the many men, like Herod, who wanted to abandon their wives. In that culture, women had no rights and the hard-hearted treated them terribly. Jesus refers the Pharisees to the creation story, which celebrates not a dominating male but a union of man and woman that is so close they are regarded as one flesh (Genesis 2:23–25).

Jesus steered people away from any system where humans seek to control others. It seems that what interested him more than convictions was what drove those convictions. In the very next passage, he talks about the most vulnerable in society, the children (Mark 10:13–16). Compassion and protection of the vulnerable are prominent values in the kingdom of God. Throughout the ages, Christians have held differing convictions about divorce. Whatever our convictions, we need to check that the compassion of Christ is a motivating influence. In this way, we can avoid having a hard heart.

Think of some of your convictions. What drives them?

MICHAEL MITTON

The beloved rich man

As he was setting out on a journey, a man ran up and knelt before him, and asked him, 'Good Teacher, what must I do to inherit eternal life?' Jesus said to him, 'Why do you call me good? No one is good but God alone. You know the commandments'... He said to [Jesus], 'Teacher, I have kept all these since my youth.' Jesus, looking at him, loved him and said, 'You lack one thing; go, sell what you own, and give the money to the poor, and you will have treasure in heaven; then come, follow me.' When he heard this, he was shocked and went away grieving, for he had many possessions.

A young man rushes up to Jesus longing to know what he must do to inherit eternal life. Jesus answers him with a strange question. Probably the man simply said 'good' teacher out of respect, but Jesus latches on to it. Only God is good, says Jesus. The man must feel a little rebuked as he hears Jesus reprise some of the ten commandments. However, he can boast that he has kept these commandments ever since he was a lad.

Then we have one of the most touching comments written by the evangelists: Jesus looked at him and loved him. Here is a poor rabbi looking on a wealthy young man with a stare of love that is directed to the heart of the matter: the man's devotion to his wealth. If you want eternal life, says Jesus, then sell everything and follow me. For what is the use of keeping all these fine commandments when you possess so much wealth but ignore the plight of the poor? The cost is too high for this young man, and he goes away in grief.

Most of us in the western world read this story with a pang of anxiety. But this is not a story to avoid. It is one in which to dwell, not least to feel the loving gaze of Christ upon us. Maybe, if the man had spent a little longer resting in that gaze of love, he could have caught a glimpse of kingdom-of-heaven treasure.

Spend some time in the gaze of Jesus' love. What does he say to you today?

MICHAEL MITTON

Servant leaders

When the ten heard this, they began to be angry with James and John. So Jesus called them and said to them, 'You know that among the Gentiles those whom they recognise as their rulers lord it over them, and their great ones are tyrants over them. But it is not so among you; but whoever wishes to become great among you must be your servant, and whoever wishes to be first among you must be slave of all. For the Son of Man came not to be served but to serve, and to give his life a ransom for many.'

In these chapters of Mark, we are seeing Jesus commending and demonstrating a kingdom-of-heaven culture that is radically different to the cultures of this world, then or now. Today's reading is a great summary of a key feature of this culture: servant leadership.

Jesus' words are sparked by another argument in the disciple camp about the nature of greatness (vv. 35–40). The disciples are still getting their notions of leadership from the prevailing culture around them. Jesus is calling them to be leaders in his kingdom, so they suppose this will involve some improvement in their status. However, Jesus teaches them a new way.

In Luke's gospel, this discussion is set in the context of the last supper (Luke 22:24–27), where Jesus states, 'I am among you as one who serves.' No doubt at some point, he referred his disciples to the prophecies in Isaiah that made it plain that the Messiah would come as a servant (Isaiah 42:1–4). Jesus demonstrates his leadership by being *among* the people in contrast to the prevailing models that lord it *over* the people.

Those who wish to lead in Christ's church are called to dwell among the people. The best leaders are the ones who relinquish power and long to see those around them flourish. A servant leader is more concerned with how others are faring than about their own position. Serving in this way is an integral part of the kingdom-of-heaven culture. This is not about being humiliated, but it is to do with choosing a humble path for the sake of empowering others.

Think of Christian leaders who have impressed you.
What has made them good leaders?

MICHAEL MITTON

Believing is seeing

When [Bartimaeus] heard that it was Jesus of Nazareth, he began to shout out and say, 'Jesus, Son of David, have mercy on me!' Many sternly ordered him to be quiet, but he cried out even more loudly, 'Son of David, have mercy on me!' Jesus stood still and said, 'Call him here.' And they called the blind man, saying to him, 'Take heart; get up, he is calling you.' So throwing off his cloak, he sprang up and came to Jesus. Then Jesus said to him, 'What do you want me to do for you?' The blind man said to him, 'My teacher, let me see again.' Jesus said to him, 'Go; your faith has made you well.' Immediately he regained his sight and followed him on the way.

We have now reached Jericho, and this is the last story before Jesus' entry into Jerusalem and his final dramatic week. We are days away from the Passover festival, when all those who lived close to Jerusalem were expected to go to the city. Those unable to would line the streets to watch the flow of pilgrims and wish them well. Jesus and his disciples are among the pilgrims passing through Jericho (Mark 10:46). Bartimaeus has clearly heard of Jesus' reputation, and he springs to life when he hears him passing. Some deep intuition tells him that Jesus is the one who can restore his sight. Once Jesus notices him, the crowd stop rebuking him and now encourage him to speak with Jesus. Bartimaeus' response to Jesus' question is simple: 'I want to see.'

Our study of these middle chapters of Mark's gospel ends with a man desperate to see, and Jesus gladly granting him his sight. It has been a common theme of these chapters – Jesus urging disciples, Pharisees, scribes, rich and poor to open their eyes to see. Here in today's story, Bartimaeus, when blind, has actually 'seen' more than many others. Jesus commends him for his faith, a faith that has roused him from the roadside to draw close to Jesus and a faith that has caused him to see everything anew and to join Jesus on this pilgrim road.

Lord Jesus, stir my soul, open my eyes and let me be a pilgrim
with you on the way today. Amen

MICHAEL MITTON

1 Corinthians 11—14

Sometimes it is tempting (especially if we are in any kind of leadership role) to wring our hands at the state of the church, whether local congregation, national denomination or worldwide body. Sometimes it is tempting to speak longingly of 'New Testament times' as a golden age when eyewitnesses to Jesus' life, death and resurrection debated as to what exactly should happen next. New worshipping communities were springing up everywhere and the wind of the Spirit blew strong. So different, we may be tempted to say, from today's squabbles.

Welcome to Corinth, a vivid example of 'dysfunctional church', as is clear from both of Paul's letters. Founded around AD50, the church's location was a city (itself only founded in 44BC) which was a leading centre of trade and full of extremely wealthy people. Civic life was ruled by profit and loss, and those values appear to have had undue influence on church life, too, with rich and poor believers treated as first- and second-class citizens. They had also got into such a mess in relation to worship that their gatherings were becoming spiritually barren, even destructive.

Paul's two lengthy epistles are a mix of firm guidance and sometimes fierce rebuke. He had to remind them of the importance of growing in wisdom and understanding, beyond the excitement of initial conversion. The Corinthian Christians had experienced the power of God's Holy Spirit; now they had to learn the disciplines of being disciples.

These four chapters of Paul's first letter include verses that are enduringly popular, quite apart from their original context. Other passages are among the most contentious parts of the Bible, continuing to cause debate and division in the present day. As we read, we can sense the fizzing energy of the newly established church and see, through Paul's eyes, how that energy ended up causing almost as many problems as it brought wonderful opportunities for witness.

While we should not idealise the early church, we can still find inspiration in its growth and creativity. As we spend time with these chapters, let us pray that the Spirit, who brought such growth and creativity back in the first century, would be at work in our own churches now.

NAOMI STARKEY

The great hat debate

Any man who prays or prophesies with something on his head disgraces his head, but any woman who prays or prophesies with her head unveiled disgraces her head… For a man ought not to have his head veiled, since he is the image and reflection of God; but woman is the reflection of man. Indeed, man was not made from woman, but woman from man… Nevertheless, in the Lord woman is not independent of man or man independent of woman. For just as woman came from man, so man comes through woman; but all things come from God.

This is one of those Bible passages that has had a disproportionate impact on church life. For generations (and still today in some denominations) these were the go-to verses that obliged women to wear hats in worship, while men had to remove them for fear of showing disrespect. The word translated as 'disgrace' has unpleasant overtones of 'shaming', the mindset that demands women (in particular) to be constantly alert lest their presence in some way causes offence. How do we begin to make a meaningful connection with this verses and the practice of our faith today?

In reading such passages, we have to bear in mind the wider historical context: this letter was written to a growing but disorderly church, sited in a lively (to put it mildly) pagan city. In the culture of the time, head coverings (or lack of) were all about social order and accountability.

New religious cults, of which Christianity would have been seen as no more than the latest example, were often associated with licentious behaviour and all kinds of excess. Here, Paul was reminding the Corinthians that they ought to live with an awareness of and respect for the surrounding social conventions. They needed to remember how others might perceive them, on the basis of something as everyday as their dress code.

That 'nevertheless' (v. 11), though, is key to understanding Paul's overall point: in Christ is found a radical freedom, which means that relationships are about mutuality, not hierarchy.

Where and how might we need to make choices that speak of accountability and good order? For example, in our use of social media?

NAOMI STARKEY

Room at the table

To begin with, when you come together as a church, I hear that there are divisions among you; and to some extent I believe it. Indeed, there have to be factions among you, for only so will it become clear who among you are genuine. When you come together, it is not really to eat the Lord's supper. For when the time comes to eat, each of you goes ahead with your own supper, and one goes hungry and another becomes drunk. What! Do you not have homes to eat and drink in? Or do you show contempt for the church of God and humiliate those who have nothing?

These verses remind us of the origins of the Eucharist: a real, rather than symbolic, 'breaking of bread', as people gathered to eat and drink together and, at some point, pause to remember the words of Jesus at the last supper. The bread and wine of the family meal became, wonderfully, tokens of the body and blood that bought salvation for the world.

That was how it was supposed to be, anyway. As Paul makes painfully clear, the Corinthian Christians were failing to demonstrate the radical hospitality and inclusive table fellowship that was meant to be at the heart of the holy feast. Instead, their worship gatherings were marked by quarrelling factions, exclusive cliques and favours for friends. As a result, the have-nots found themselves marginalised, to the point of actually going hungry, while others overindulged. There may have been practical reasons involved: churches gathered in private homes and as numbers grew, so space (and the best seats) became highly sought after.

The familiar is always more comfortable and newcomers (especially newcomers very different from ourselves) can prove challenging to accommodate. Discrimination can be subtle and veiled by a veneer of 'this is how we do things here', but still felt keenly by the one discriminated against.

Paul's stark words continue to speak to us: it is better not to come to worship at all than to turn up and, through our attitudes and actions, exclude others.

How might our worship – and fellowship gatherings – be at risk
of excluding others? What changes might we need to make to avoid that?

NAOMI STARKEY

A loaf of bread, a cup of wine

For I received from the Lord what I also handed on to you, that the Lord Jesus on the night when he was betrayed took a loaf of bread, and when he had given thanks, he broke it and said, 'This is my body that is for you. Do this in remembrance of me.' In the same way he took the cup also, after supper, saying, 'This cup is the new covenant in my blood. Do this, as often as you drink it, in remembrance of me.' For as often as you eat this bread and drink the cup, you proclaim the Lord's death until he comes.

The opening sentence here underlines how young the church was when 1 Corinthians was written. Paul was not present in the upper room on the night before Jesus died, but those world-changing days lay just a few years in the past. There were still eyewitnesses around to shape the life and witness of the congregations growing around the Mediterranean (and beginning to reach beyond).

The words of Jesus recorded here are one of four slightly different versions of what are known as the 'words of institution' found in the Bible. They continue to be spoken and shared week by week in different languages, different liturgies and the many different variants of the church, some of whom (sadly) do not recognise the validity of others.

We do well to reflect, often, on the simplicity of the act of Communion: bread, wine and the words of Jesus about remembering his offering of himself. Much of what may be added (as human tradition rather than divine command) may be helpful if it aids understanding and deepens worship, but unhelpful if it distracts from or obscures the fundamental accessibility of the Eucharist.

Sharing this holy meal is about far more than remembering, as Paul points out. In our eating and drinking, we are proclaiming the truth at the heart of our faith: the one who died for our sins and rose again to defeat death will come again in glory. For that we wait, we hope and we pray.

What might be involved in 'decluttering' the worship of your local church?

NAOMI STARKEY

Being together, belonging together

Whoever, therefore, eats the bread or drinks the cup of the Lord in an unworthy manner will be answerable for the body and blood of the Lord. Examine yourselves, and only then eat of the bread and drink of the cup. For all who eat and drink without discerning the body, eat and drink judgement against themselves. For this reason many of you are weak and ill, and some have died... So then, my brothers and sisters, when you come together to eat, wait for one another. If you are hungry, eat at home, so that when you come together, it will not be for your condemnation.

Never one to mince words when there was an important matter at stake, Paul's bluntness is shocking: if your behaviour makes a mockery of the holy act of Communion, you are counted as among those who put Christ to death. The Corinthians' drinking and eating will bring judgement, not grace, and such judgement can already be observed, Paul says, in their recent experiences of ill health and even death.

We may respond that modern science and medical understanding has done away with such attitudes. Indeed, they were challenged during Jesus' ministry, in the healing of the man born blind when the disciples had assumed wrongdoing by his parents (see John 9).

Words from the Book of Common Prayer confession nudge us to admit a wider perspective: 'We have left undone those things which we ought to have done; and we have done those things which we ought not to have done, and there is no health in us.' Selfish, unkind behaviour, whether towards those different from us or towards our nearest and dearest, does not lead to peace of mind and wholeness of heart. In recent years, research and experience have shown how physical resilience and mental well-being are linked, and mental well-being is generally boosted by a mindset characterised by positivity, generosity and kindness. None of those qualities were evident in the worship of the Corinthian church, hence Paul's stern warning.

It is temptingly easy to identify negative behaviour in other people.
It is harder to pray, with the psalmist, 'See if there is any wicked way in me,
and lead me in the way everlasting' (Psalm 139:24).

NAOMI STARKEY

Getting it right

Now concerning spiritual gifts, brothers and sisters, I do not want you to be uninformed… I want you to understand that no one speaking by the Spirit of God ever says 'Let Jesus be cursed!' and no one can say 'Jesus is Lord' except by the Holy Spirit. Now there are varieties of gifts, but the same Spirit; and there are varieties of services, but the same Lord; and there are varieties of activities, but it is the same God who activates all of them in everyone. To each is given the manifestation of the Spirit for the common good.

It is helpful sometimes to pause and reflect on how fragile the early church was. Subject to random outbreaks of persecution, scattered among the indifferent or hostile provinces around the Mediterranean, the little communities struggled to build a common life without the benefit of trained leaders, established creeds or an agreed set of teaching documents. Paul's letters to the churches in his care had to combine encouragement and explanation with reprimand, as he tried to disciple them from afar.

One challenge was ensuring that the followers of Jesus stayed distinct from the esoteric religious cults which were popular then. Here, Paul is trying to help the Corinthian Christians discern what was 'of God' and what was merely human invention. However strongly a speaker might feel that they had to utter certain words, the Spirit of God would never inspire something contrary to the life-giving message of salvation, the saving love of Christ.

Clearly, the church in Corinth was experiencing an outpouring of God's grace, being blessed with gifts including wisdom and knowledge, faith, discernment, healing and utterances in 'various kinds of tongues' (v. 10). However exciting the times though, Paul emphasised to them the fundamental importance of everything being 'for the common good'. That was the standard against which every spiritual urge had to be tested. Their focus should always be worshipping God, not promoting their own spiritual stature.

How do those responsible for the worship, prayer and preaching in our congregations make sure they combine the necessary competence with appropriate humility? How do we balance aiming for excellence with encouraging people to explore their own, perhaps unexpected gifts?

NAOMI STARKEY

Needing each other

Just as the body is one and has many members, and all the members of the body, though many, are one body, so it is with Christ. For in the one Spirit we were all baptised into one body... and we were all made to drink of one Spirit. Indeed, the body does not consist of one member but of many. If the foot were to say, 'Because I am not a hand, I do not belong to the body', that would not make it any less a part of the body... If one member suffers, all suffer together with it; if one member is honoured, all rejoice together with it.

We are probably familiar with the notion of the modern world as individualistic. It can be startling, then, to realise that the church in Corinth, more than two millennia ago, was prone to the same attitude. Paul had to remind them repeatedly that they needed one another. More than that, their lives were (whether they accepted it or not) bound intimately together and could not, should not, flourish or fail alone.

Such ties of interdependence are hard to develop and arguably harder to maintain. Organising our lives to avoid awkward relationships and angular encounters is so much easier. As sisters and brothers in Christ, we have to hold tight to the knowledge that, through the Spirit's work, we have been made one body; the idea that we can manage alone is in fact illusion. It is not about 'having to go to church to be a Christian'; it is about belonging together being a fundamental mark of discipleship.

As in any kind of family, so in the family of the church: members have to learn to disagree well, negotiating the inevitable disagreements. As in any kind of family, too, members have to resolve to live together with compassion, sensitive to one another's weaknesses rather than exploiting them. Individual fulfilment has to be held in tension with the common good, not to stifle personal expression but to sustain the bonds of love.

'No one is an island, entire of itself; everyone is a part of the continent, a part of the main' (John Donne, 1572–1631, adapted).

NAOMI STARKEY

No second best

Now you are the body of Christ and individually members of it. And God has appointed in the church first apostles, second prophets, third teachers; then deeds of power, then gifts of healing, forms of assistance, forms of leadership, various kinds of tongues. Are all apostles? Are all prophets? Are all teachers? Do all work miracles? Do all possess gifts of healing? Do all speak in tongues? Do all interpret? But strive for the greater gifts. And I will show you a still more excellent way.

So, Paul says, you belong together, as much as the limbs of the body 'belong' to the heart. That doesn't mean you have lost your individual identity; but it does mean that no member should consider themselves more or less important than others. Nor should they value some spiritual gifts more than others. Each gift, as each member, has merit and a part to play in the whole.

That is a principle easier to say (or write) than to put into practice. Inevitably, gifts connected with any kind of 'up front' role are treated as premium. 'Deeds of power' sounds more impressive than 'forms of assistance', for example, but anyone who has been in a well-functioning team, whether in the office or on the playing field, will know first-hand the importance of striking a balance between unity and diversity.

Inevitably some gifts will be more significant than others at certain times in the life of a congregation. Paul seems to admit this when he speaks of apostles, followed by prophets and then teachers. People need to come to faith before they can grow in faith; a church has to be established before it can be maintained.

We should note, though, that he also urges the Corinthians to 'strive for the greater gifts'. Discipleship is the journey of a lifetime (and beyond), and there is always more work for our Father to do in us and for us. At the same time, we are speaking of 'gifts', not 'awards'; God blesses us freely, through no deserving or merit of our own.

What spiritual gifts can you identify in your own life? What 'greater gift' would you like to 'strive' for?

NAOMI STARKEY

The more excellent way

If I speak in the tongues of mortals and of angels, but do not have love, I am a noisy gong or a clanging cymbal. And if I have prophetic powers, and understand all mysteries and all knowledge, and if I have all faith, so as to remove mountains, but do not have love, I am nothing. If I give away all my possessions, and if I hand over my body so that I may boast, but do not have love, I gain nothing.

Following the best rhetorical practice of his time, Paul now pauses in his carefully crafted argument about spiritual gifts and embarks on what has become famous as his 'hymn to love'. Using repetition and flowing cadences, he will build to a climax of poetry over 13 verses; it is no surprise that this chapter is a favourite choice for weddings.

In this opening section, he refers back to some of the gifts mentioned previously: 'tongues of angels', 'prophetic powers', 'all faith', all of which the Corinthians had eagerly sought. But, says Paul, love is more important than even these spectacular manifestations, because without love the grandest spiritual gestures end up as mere show. He also speaks of the kind of heroic acts of self-sacrifice that are not unknown even today. Back in the first century, with martyrdom an ever-present threat, such acts would have been the stuff of hushed tones but, says Paul, if your life is not suffused with love, even they lose their power.

There is no place in God's kingdom for hard-hearted showmanship. There is no place for calculating hypocrisy or clinging to power at all costs, nor for shoring up personal position at the expense of others. We follow a servant king, who washed his friends' feet, who gave up everything 'to seek and to save that which was lost' (Luke 19:10, KJV). Without love, no matter how important we are in the eyes of the world (or the eyes of the church), we are 'nothing'.

Who is the godliest person that you know (or know of)? What is it about them that compels respect? How far would you describe them as characterised by love?

NAOMI STARKEY

Love is... and is not...

Love is patient; love is kind; love is not envious or boastful or arrogant or rude. It does not insist on its own way; it is not irritable or resentful; it does not rejoice in wrongdoing, but rejoices in the truth. It bears all things, believes all things, hopes all things, endures all things. Love never ends. But as for prophecies, they will come to an end; as for tongues, they will cease; as for knowledge, it will come to an end. For we know only in part, and we prophesy only in part; but when the complete comes, the partial will come to an end.

Some people reading today's passage will remember the long-running 'Love is...' cartoons, which originated in a series of love notes by cartoonist Kim Casali for her future husband. Paul, though, tells us not only what love is, but also what love is not, balancing patience, kindness and joy with the reality of human relationships, which are so often marked by very different behaviour. Even so, he says, the resilience of love means that it can 'endure all things', never losing grip on hope. We may know from personal experience how human love can in fact falter and fail; the love described here is found in its fullest flowering in the love of the Father for us, his children.

Mentioning again the spiritual gifts which were the focus of the previous chapter, Paul emphasises, with threefold repetition, how even the most impressive of such gifts will one day cease to be. They are only partial because they operate within a partial, mortal world that can contain no more than a glimpse of the glory of God's kingdom.

This may remind us of the sobering stories that emerge from time to time of those hailed as 'spiritual giants' during their lifetime, who are later revealed to have used and abused others for their own gratification. Despite authority, influence and all kinds of accomplishment, their hearts turn out to be devoid of love. Ultimately their gifts prove to have been wasted.

Ask yourself to complete (without over-thinking!) the sentence 'Love is...'
What words came to mind and why?

NAOMI STARKEY

Deeper into the mystery

For we know only in part, and we prophesy only in part; but when the complete comes, the partial will come to an end. When I was a child, I spoke like a child, I thought like a child, I reasoned like a child; when I became an adult, I put an end to childish ways. For now we see in a mirror, dimly, but then we will see face to face. Now I know only in part; then I will know fully, even as I have been fully known. And now faith, hope, and love abide, these three; and the greatest of these is love.

The chapter reaches a crescendo as the poetic phrases ring out one after another, taking us deeper into the mystery of love. Learning how love is the heartbeat of the universe is the journey of a lifetime, a revelation that will only become entirely clear 'then' (which may either be in God's presence or just through the passing of the years of our lives). A comparison is made with growing to maturity: 'childish ways' are not foolish in themselves but simply the sign of a life in formation. When that process of formation is complete, the 'childish ways' no longer have a place. They have (all being well) been replaced by the wisdom that comes through experience.

The journey is not just about our own seeing and knowing; it also concerns being 'fully known'. Nothing can be hidden from God, not even our most secret selves. We should also reflect that, however carefully we try to control the way we appear to others, our true character will eventually become clear. If we cultivate mercy and kindness, or bitterness and judgement, that is how we risk being remembered, at least by those whom we have injured.

'And now', says Paul, let me bring you back to the basics. There is faith and there is hope, two virtues that will make for a secure and steadfast life. And then there is love, without which everything else will fall apart. Thus the hymn to love is concluded, the teacher draws breath and, in the following verses, shows how it all fits together.

What do you most long to 'know fully'? What steps can you take now that will lead to such knowing?

NAOMI STARKEY

The point of worship

Pursue love and strive for the spiritual gifts, and especially that you may prophesy. For those who speak in a tongue do not speak to other people but to God; for nobody understands them… On the other hand, those who prophesy speak to other people for their building up and encouragement and consolation… If I come to you speaking in tongues, how will I benefit you unless I speak to you in some revelation or knowledge or prophecy or teaching?… Since you are eager for spiritual gifts, strive to excel in them for building up the church.

So, says Paul, I hope I have persuaded you of the importance of love. Make that the foundation and the true purpose for worship to emerge, which is (in a word) 'connection'. Worship obviously connects the individual worshipper to God but it should also connect individuals together as the body of Christ, which is the church. And for connection to take place, worship has to involve at least a measure of mutual understanding.

The Corinthian church was relatively new and bursting with enthusiasm. Unfortunately, in their enthusiasm, they were forgetting to ensure that everyone felt included. Ecstatic worship might bless the individual but leave others at a loss unless explanation and interpretation were provided. Paul also feared that the believers in Corinth were focusing too much on what they considered the 'best' gifts, so that worship risked becoming a kind of contest for who was the holiest.

Prophecy, by contrast, is presented as a much more useful gift. This may sound surprising, as the popular image of 'prophet' is somebody waving a placard, warning that 'the end is nigh'. In fact the Bible usually speaks of prophecy as what we might call 'forth-telling' rather than 'fore-telling'. Instead of predicting the future, it is more to do with prayerfully discerning realities that may be overlooked or obscured by the everyday. When these realities are discerned, they can, with wise and sensitive reflection, bring clarity to otherwise difficult situations, and, as with all spiritual gifts, help to build the church.

How might the worship in your church benefit from regular or occasional explanation to help everybody feel part of what goes on?

NAOMI STARKEY

Learning together

One who speaks in a tongue should pray for the power to interpret. For if I pray in a tongue, my spirit prays but my mind is unproductive. What should I do then? I will pray with the spirit, but I will pray with the mind also; I will sing praise with the spirit, but I will sing praise with the mind also. Otherwise, if you say a blessing with the spirit, how can anyone in the position of an outsider say the 'Amen' to your thanksgiving, since the outsider does not know what you are saying? For you may give thanks well enough, but the other person is not built up.

Worship is not only about connecting with God and with one another, it is a means of spiritual growth. We do not praise God because God is needy for praise but because we want to express our love and gratitude to our Father in heaven. That outpouring of love and gratitude blesses us as we express it, but the experience of blessing does not negate the importance of engaging the mind with what is happening!

Paul holds tightly to his point, wanting to make absolutely sure that the Corinthian believers understand: worship must involve both spirit and mind, heart and head. It must be more than a 'sugar rush' of joy; it has to be part of lifelong transformation. Only then will the believers continue in their journey towards maturity. Only then can their church community hope to endure the challenges of first-century life and carry on into the future.

These days, people tend to pick a church to attend according to a number of issues besides proximity, including worship style, quality of preaching and warmth of fellowship. Simply supporting the nearest local church is (in my experience anyway) more a feature of small town or village life. There are advantages and disadvantages with both ways of choosing, but one distinct advantage of 'going local' is that we learn to negotiate and navigate difference, in terms of personalities and our personal preferences. Such coming together can be immeasurably enriching, not only for the individual but for the community as a whole.

How do you choose where to worship? What are your priorities in choosing – and how have those priorities changed over time?

NAOMI STARKEY

A plan for worship

When you come together, each one has a hymn, a lesson, a revelation, a tongue, or an interpretation. Let all things be done for building up. If anyone speaks in a tongue, let there be only two or at most three, and each in turn; and let one interpret… Let two or three prophets speak, and let the others weigh what is said. If a revelation is made to someone else sitting nearby, let the first person be silent… And the spirits of prophets are subject to the prophets, for God is a God not of disorder but of peace.

Here Paul offers some practical advice on how to order worship so that everyone is involved and good relationships are maintained within the congregation. First there is the reminder that worship should be about 'building up', lest anyone fall into the trap of using it as a way of showing off their giftedness. He also urges them to preserve order ('peace') rather than relinquish all control, thereby risking letting themselves be overwhelmed by spiritual ecstasy.

Whether our worship is high or low, liturgical or spontaneous, lay-led or a more traditional 'Father knows best' approach, we need to work for balance. The Spirit moves where the Spirit wills (see John 3:8) and there will be times when our worship should be able to 'breathe the breath of God', instead of moving briskly on to the next item. At the same time, wise and sensitive leadership can help channel emotion within worship, so that it acts to build up individuals and church community alike. This is Paul's plea to the Corinthians.

And always, in our worship, we should remember that our praise, Sunday by Sunday, is just a faint echo of the praise that rises in the throne room of heaven, where we too will one day stand in the Father's presence.

'There was a great multitude that no one could count, from every nation, from all tribes and peoples and languages, standing before the throne and before the Lamb, robed in white, with palm branches in their hands. They cried in a loud voice, saying, "Salvation belongs to our God who is seated on the throne, and to the Lamb!"' (Revelation 7:9–10)

NAOMI STARKEY

Be quiet!

(As in all the churches of the saints, women should be silent in the churches. For they are not permitted to speak, but should be subordinate, as the law also says. If there is anything they desire to know, let them ask their husbands at home. For it is shameful for a woman to speak in church. Or did the word of God originate with you? Or are you the only ones it has reached?) Anyone who claims to be a prophet, or to have spiritual powers, must acknowledge that what I am writing to you is a command of the Lord.

We finish as we started, with a passage that sounds more intemperate than Paul's earlier comments in chapter 11. Some would argue that we should reject these verses as a later addition that had nothing to do with the apostle. Others seize them as conclusive proof that allowing women leadership roles in church is against the teaching of scripture.

As at the beginning of these readings, we have to reflect not only on the original context but on how to make sense of Paul's words today. Contextually it is helpful to remember that New Testament letters often represented half of an ongoing conversation. We do not have the replies (although we can sometimes find hints in the letters themselves). We do not know exactly what was going on in the church in Corinth but do know that keeping order was at times difficult. Maybe that offers some explanation for Paul's disapproving tone here?

We can also be reminded that the process of change is rarely, if ever, smooth. Sometimes those who are impatient for new things can feel that they have waited long enough. They decide to press ahead with their plans, without much regard for the consequences. Such revolutionary approaches (while often understandable) can cause much collateral damage.

As any fitness enthusiast knows, changing the physical body takes effort and time, if injury is to be avoided. The demanding call of Christ for the church is to live as one body; we should aim (where possible) for transformation which, while perhaps not pain-free, will not be destructive either.

Women's voices are now heard in leadership in the lives of most churches; what other groups remain little-heard or even silenced?

NAOMI STARKEY

Summer

It is summer in the northern hemisphere. (If you are reading this on the other side of the world you will be able to imagine.) The British Isles have turned to face the sun, and the days are blessed with warmth and long hours of sunlight. Warmth and light are the hallmarks of summer, and we respond to this by using our leisure time differently, spending more of it outdoors.

'For everything there is a season, and a time for every matter under heaven' (Ecclesiastes 3:1, NRSV). Summer is the season for music in the park, drinks in the garden, holidays and long shadows on the sports field; it is a time for picnics, barbecues, ice cream and warm sand under bare feet.

The eye of faith sees God in everything. So summer is not just something that we experience, an astronomical phenomenon that simply 'happens'. God is present in summer just as God is present in everything, because God made it and made it for a purpose. All things in heaven and on earth, visible and invisible, were created *in* Christ and *by* Christ, *through* Christ and *for* Christ, as the great hymn of Colossians 1:15–20 tells us. Or, as John the Evangelist would later encapsulate it: 'All things came into being through him, and without him not one thing came into being' (John 1:3).

In the natural world, summer is the season of growth – the abundant and generous growth of grain, vegetables, flowers and summer fruits. In the UK the growing season is short: only four months can be guaranteed frost-free, perhaps even less in the far north. Much of our food is grown in this small window of opportunity, not only on farms but also in countless gardens and allotments. Modern freezing and canning techniques mean it can now be stored and supplied all year round, which of course wasn't the case in biblical times when fewer and less effective preserving methods existed. Famine was never far away.

But enough of that for now. It is 'summertime, and the livin' is easy', as the George Gershwin song from *Porgy and Bess* goes. So let's look out for signs of God's presence and his holy hand at work as we explore the theme of summer through a Christian lens over the next two weeks.

TIM HEATON

God's summer

Yet God my King is from of old, working salvation in the earth. You divided the sea by your might; you broke the heads of the dragons in the waters. You crushed the heads of Leviathan; you gave him as food for the creatures of the wilderness. You cut openings for springs and torrents; you dried up ever-flowing streams. Yours is the day, yours also the night; you established the luminaries and the sun. You have fixed all the bounds of the earth; you made summer and winter.

Here is the science: the earth's orbit around the sun is not a perfect circle; it's elliptic, or slightly oval-shaped, though this is not what causes seasons. The point in the 365-day orbit where the earth is closest to the sun occurs in January, and the furthest point in July. So we are actually as far away from the sun now as we ever are. The reason it is summer has to do with the tilt of the earth on its axis: as the earth moves around its orbit, first one and then the other hemisphere is tipped towards the sun, thereby experiencing summer.

This is the mechanism by which God 'made summer' (v. 17). Science explains what the psalmist could only perceive through faith. Science and religion do not contradict each other, they complement one another. Albert Einstein once said, 'Science without religion is lame; religion without science is blind.' Science gives us remarkable insights into the workings of the universe and helps us to understand the great mysteries of God's creation, while religion offers an explanation more profound than that which science alone can provide.

The seasons allow every part of God's world to share in the beauty of change, and to enjoy the varied blessings of light and dark, heat and cold, growth and dormancy. The 'Land of Always Winter' exists only in fantasy tales, because God made summer and winter. No part of the earth is permanently dark, permanently cold and permanently dormant. The whole planet from pole to pole supports life. Even the Arctic enjoys a summer, thanks be to God.

God of the seasons, creator and sustainer of the universe, thank you for summer and for all the joy, beauty and blessings that it brings. Amen

TIM HEATON

The promise of summer

'From the fig tree learn its lesson: as soon as its branch becomes tender and puts forth its leaves, you know that summer is near. So also, when you see these things taking place, you know that he is near, at the very gates. Truly I tell you, this generation will not pass away until all these things have taken place. Heaven and earth will pass away, but my words will not pass away.'

The fig tree is indigenous to the eastern Mediterranean region, where its bud burst heralds the approach of summer. If I had to name a harbinger of summer in the UK, I suppose it would be our native hawthorn, also known as the may tree, an ancient symbol of new life, fertility and rebirth, whose branches blossom in spring and were once woven into May Day crowns. Shakespeare's 'darling buds of May' of Sonnet 18 ('Shall I compare thee to a summer's day?'), might refer to the hawthorn rather than to the month.

The Palestine of Jesus' time was an agrarian society and the images he used often sprang from the natural world around him. Figs, grapes and olives were widely cultivated, and they inspired many parables and proverbs. As well as its eponymous fruit, the Mount of Olives was famous for its fig trees, which sometimes attained a height of 30 feet. When the fig tree becomes green, one can be certain not only that summer is coming but also that it is near.

Jesus draws a parallel here to his return. 'These things taking place' (v. 29) refers to the 'desolating sacrilege' (i.e. the desecration of the temple) and the subsequent end-time turmoil of verses 14–23, and Jesus reassures his hearers, 'I will be near.' Just as the leafing of the fig tree is a sure sign of the proximity of summer, so 'these things taking place' will signal that the day of salvation is near. This is about certainty as well as imminence. Contemporary society seems to be less sure about God's promises than it used to be, but from the fig tree can learn its lesson.

God of the fig tree, whose lifeblood pulses through its branches and brings forth its leaves, keep us alert to the signs of your coming. Amen

TIM HEATON

Summer plenty

Therefore keep the commandments of the Lord your God, by walking in his ways and by fearing him. For the Lord your God is bringing you into a good land, a land with flowing streams, with springs and underground waters welling up in valleys and hills, a land of wheat and barley, of vines and fig trees and pomegranates, a land of olive trees and honey, a land where you may eat bread without scarcity, where you will lack nothing... You shall eat your fill and bless the Lord your God for the good land that he has given you.

A colony of honeybees has swarmed and taken up residence in the apple tree, hanging in a bulbous cluster around their queen. It is a common summertime phenomenon, and they will soon move on. Scout bees will already be out searching for a more suitable home, but a beekeeper is coming to collect them before they find one. They are a valuable commodity and their honey a prized foodstuff, just as it was in the promised land (v. 8).

Canaan, we are told twice, is a 'good land' (vv. 7, 10) where the Israelites will want for nothing. They are instructed not to forget the Lord their God; they are to keep his commandments and walk in his ways. God has delivered them from slavery in Egypt and is about to bring them into a 'land flowing with milk and honey' (Exodus 3:8). When the little they have now has been multiplied many times over – their herds and their flocks, their fruit and their grain – they must never forget God in their prosperity.

Summer is the season of plenty. The abundance of everything in nature we see around us today is a reminder of God's lavish goodness and kindness. In our own good land, we often eat our fill but forget to bless the Lord our God. It is easy for an affluent lifestyle to encourage pride and for wealth to inspire self-importance, but we should remember that life is ordered and sustained by God and all our riches are derived from his power.

Generous God, provider of plenty, may we never forget that we prosper only by your grace, and that all our bounty comes from you alone. Amen

TIM HEATON

A heavenly summer

Then he led me back along the bank of the river. As I came back, I saw on the bank of the river a great many trees on one side and on the other. He said to me, 'This water flows towards the eastern region and goes down into the Arabah; and when it enters the sea, the sea of stagnant waters, the water will become fresh... On the banks, on both sides of the river, there will grow all kinds of trees for food. Their leaves will not wither nor their fruit fail, but they will bear fresh fruit every month, because the water for them flows from the sanctuary. Their fruit will be for food, and their leaves for healing.'

If spring symbolises hope, summer symbolises joy; if spring is resurrection, summer is eternal life. There is abundance and plenty, a foretaste of the heavenly banquet. Surely there is something heavenly about summer in myriad ways: a swim in the sea, strawberries and cream, an al fresco meal on a warm evening. Eternity itself would not be long enough for days such as these! This is resurrection life, life in all its fullness.

In a vision, Ezekiel travels to Jerusalem and receives a tour of the new temple. His guide shows him water flowing out from beneath the temple towards the east, the flow becoming a stream and the stream turning into a river. The trees on the fertile riverbanks are prolific and fruitful, bearing fruit every month of the year and with leaves that never wither. The leaves have a purpose: they are herbal, medicinal and healing.

It is a vision echoed in Revelation 22. In that vision of the New Jerusalem, John sees the river of the water of life flowing from the throne of God through the middle of the holy city, and on either side is the tree of life, with its twelve kinds of fruit and leaves for the healing of the nations. There is year-round fruitfulness from deciduous trees whose leaves never turn colour and fall. This is eternal summer; this is our promised land.

Eternal and ever-loving God, provider and healer of all, help us to fix our eyes on you and on our true home in heaven. Amen

TIM HEATON

Summer harvest

He also said, 'The kingdom of God is as if someone would scatter seed on the ground, and would sleep and rise night and day, and the seed would sprout and grow, he does not know how. The earth produces of itself, first the stalk, then the head, then the full grain in the head. But when the grain is ripe, at once he goes in with his sickle, because the harvest has come.'

Spring is seedtime; summer is harvest. I was raised in a small village surrounded by enormous fields of wheat and barley, and when I was a teenager, during the summer holidays I would help to bring in the harvest, mostly doing the mundane work of loading bales of straw on to trailers and unloading them in a barn. Come August, the sight of giant machines working in these fields of gold all over the countryside will be for many the typical image of modern harvest.

The parable of the growing seed highlights the miracle of nature contained within such a tiny organism. It is truly miraculous (from the Latin *miraculum*, an 'object of wonder') that something apparently so lifeless and inert can sprout and grow. All it needs is warm earth, light and moisture. The Swedish botanist Carl Linnaeus once said, 'Find wonder in everything, even the most commonplace,' and the germination of a seed is certainly something to marvel at.

The strangely passive sower and reaper in the parable is God. We are told that human actions can neither hasten nor delay the coming of the kingdom. The kingdom *will come* because that is God's plan and purpose. Like the harvest, which stems from next-to-invisible beginnings, it is certain; God will see to that. Yet the apparent lack of any human agency during the process does not mean we can sit back and do nothing and leave it all to God. God works through people, and we are called to be kingdom-growers so that others may have life. And if our testimony to the gospel may at times appear insignificant or even fruitless, we should never be discouraged and never give up.

Gathering God, bring to fruition the work of your kingdom, and make us part of that joyful harvest in which your loving purpose is completed. Amen

TIM HEATON

Summer flowers

'And why do you worry about clothing? Consider the lilies of the field, how they grow; they neither toil nor spin, yet I tell you, even Solomon in all his glory was not clothed like one of these. But if God so clothes the grass of the field, which is alive today and tomorrow is thrown into the oven, will he not much more clothe you – you of little faith? Therefore do not worry, saying, 'What will we eat?' or 'What will we drink?' or 'What will we wear?'

The goldfinches are eating the seed heads of the hawksbeard in the wild-flower garden, great flocks of them descending and balancing precariously on the wavering stalks. It is the season of plenty for wildlife too. I have a passion for our native wildflowers – plants as God created them, not modified by plant breeders for greater stature, vigour, colour or scent. I also have a sneaking suspicion that our native bees, bugs and butterflies prefer them too.

The 'lilies of the field' (v. 28) could refer to any of the beautiful wildflowers of the Palestinian countryside. Such flowers abound in our fields, public parks and roadside verges too, but unlike Jesus many people hardly notice them. Right now there is hedge woundwort, bird's-foot trefoil and self-heal – red, yellow and blue together – the primary colours of God's palette. Yes, even Solomon, the third king of Israel who acquired legendary wealth through manufacturing, overseas trading and other commercial ventures, was not clothed like one of these.

Lady's bedstraw is flowering now. The story goes that the manger in the stable at Bethlehem was empty because the animals had eaten all the hay, so Mary laid the baby Jesus on a bed of these beautiful yellow flowers. All the natural world is God's handiwork; how fitting it is that much of it tells the Christian story. But how it must grieve the heart of God that so much of it today is marred by litter and pollution. We must work harder to protect creation and to improve biodiversity and the health of ecosystems. God made it and loves it, and so must we.

God of all the flowers of the field, thank you for the beauty of everything you have made; forgive us the damage we do. Amen

TIM HEATON

Summer birds

How lovely is your dwelling place, O Lord of hosts! My soul longs, indeed it faints for the courts of the Lord; my heart and my flesh sing for joy to the living God. Even the sparrow finds a home, and the swallow a nest for herself, where she may lay her young, at your altars, O Lord of hosts, my King and my God. Happy are those who live in your house, ever singing your praise.

The swallows were out early this morning, riding the high currents, mouths open like nets to catch their insect breakfast. The swallow is a summer visitor to northern Europe and the Mediterranean region. They have migrated here all the way from southern Africa, a journey of 6,000 miles, covered at the rate of 200 a day. They have crossed the Congo rainforest, the Sahara desert, Morocco, Spain and France, an epic journey that takes a month. To Palestine, they fly a more easterly route via the Red Sea.

The sparrow, on the other hand, is an indigenous species both here and in Israel. Psalm 84 therefore speaks of resident and migrant together, native and foreigner living peaceably as one. Both find sanctuary in the temple and joy in the presence of God. Sparrows were quite literally two-a-penny in Jesus' day, but God still knew and cared about what happened to them (Matthew 10:29). In the UK today, the house sparrow is red-listed as a species of high conservation concern.

The sad truth is there are far fewer birds of many different species around than there used to be. Over the past 50 years, according to the RSPB, 40 million birds have vanished from British skies. Including mammals as well, around two-fifths of all UK species are in decline. We must take this trend seriously, for God's sake. 'I know all the birds of the air, and all that moves in the field is mine,' says the Lord (Psalm 50:11). Nature needs our help now like never before, and we must do everything in our power to protect God's creatures. For one swallow doesn't make a summer.

God of all the birds of the air, no sparrow falls to the ground unnoticed by you; help us to care as much as you do. Amen

TIM HEATON

Summer holidays

The Lord spoke to Moses, saying… For six days shall work be done; but the seventh day is a sabbath of complete rest, a holy convocation; you shall do no work: it is a sabbath to the Lord throughout your settlements. These are the appointed festivals of the Lord, the holy convocations, which you shall celebrate at the time appointed for them. In the first month, on the fourteenth day of the month, at twilight, there shall be a passover-offering to the Lord, and on the fifteenth day of the same month is the festival of unleavened bread to the Lord; for seven days you shall eat unleavened bread.

We are going on holiday today. I can safely predict this more than a year in advance, because my wife and I are creatures of habit. We always travel to the Lake District on this Sunday before our wedding anniversary, and always to the same hotel. It has become a home-from-home, where we spend a week walking on the high fells and mountaintops, or along the river valleys and around the lakes, depending on the weather, refreshing and recharging our bodies, minds and spirits.

Our word 'holiday' originates from 'holy day'. The Hebrew 'festivals of the Lord' (v. 4) were days or periods of religious joy. Many of them coincided with the seasons and the cycle of the agricultural year, and by these festivals the Israelites acknowledged God as their provider. The 'festival of unleavened bread' (v. 6) became the perennial commemoration of their deliverance from slavery in Egypt, the Passover itself commencing after sunset on the day of the first full moon of spring.

Public holidays in the UK remain mostly connected to our Christian festivals, notably Christmas and Easter, and the spring bank holiday continues to bear testimony to Whit Monday (Pentecost). Summer is the season for extended breaks from work and school, a time for rest and recreation when the weather is kind. We know that Jesus took time out from healing and proclaiming the kingdom, to escape the gruelling demands of his work; I hope that you can too.

God of sabbath rest, we give thanks for the gift of holidays and for all who make them possible, also remembering those who are unable to.

TIM HEATON

Summer sun

He also said, 'With what can we compare the kingdom of God, or what parable will we use for it? It is like a mustard seed, which, when sown upon the ground, is the smallest of all the seeds on earth; yet when it is sown it grows up and becomes the greatest of all shrubs, and puts forth large branches, so that the birds of the air can make nests in its shade.' With many such parables he spoke the word to them, as they were able to hear it.

The sun is beating down. Walking out the front door is like stepping off an aeroplane in Athens: the heat hits you like an oven. We seek the shade when outside, perhaps even the cool of the church. July often sees the hottest temperatures in the UK, the record (at the time of going to press) being 40.3°C at Coningsby, Lincolnshire, on 19 July 2022. Too hot for most, it is a long way off the 54.4°C recorded in Death Valley, California, at the National Park's Furnace Creek Visitor Centre on 9 July 2021.

The parable of the mustard seed has a meaning that is often missed. We know well the main point that it makes, that great things come from small beginnings. Tiny seeds grow into huge plants, and while the emergence of the seed may go unnoticed the fully grown plant will be unmissable. So it is with the kingdom of God. Yet the parable also tells us that the mustard bush has a function, providing shelter from the sun for the birds that make nests in its shade. The 'greatest of all shrubs' (v. 32) has a purpose: it is there for others.

Kingdom greatness is far-removed from the so-called 'greatness' of worldly empires. God's kingdom does not replicate the importance that self-serving earthly nations attempt to build. The kingdom of God is for others. And God does not give the gift of faith – or the secret of the kingdom – to individuals as their own private possession: it is a gift that must provide for others. So let us try to grow the kingdom, slowly but surely, one mustard seed at a time.

God and king of the universe, grant that we may sow a seed that will become a blessing for others. Amen

TIM HEATON

Summer rain

Elijah went up to the top of Carmel; there he bowed himself down upon the earth and put his face between his knees. He said to his servant, 'Go up now, look towards the sea.' He went up and looked, and said, 'There is nothing.' Then he said, 'Go again seven times.' At the seventh time he said, 'Look, a little cloud no bigger than a person's hand is rising out of the sea.' Then he said, 'Go and say to Ahab, "Harness your chariot and go down before the rain stops you."' In a little while the heavens grew black with clouds and wind; there was heavy rain.

'Three fine days and a thunderstorm' is the famous definition of an English summer attributed to King George II in 1730. Summer thunderstorms can be very violent, bringing torrential rain, hailstones, lightning and squally winds. We would hardly ever regard them as welcome, but in the lands of the Bible, where drought can be prolonged, heavy rain is something they pray for and give thanks to God when it comes. It is heaven sent and a blessing to be counted.

Elijah brings to an end a three-year drought in Israel. King Ahab, after marrying Jezebel, had begun to worship Baal, the Canaanite storm god believed to be responsible for bringing the yearly rains that restored fertility to the land. To prove that it is God who controls rain and drought, fertility and sterility, life and death, Elijah announces that God has withheld the rains (1 Kings 17:1). Once the people have acknowledged that there is only one God in Israel, Elijah speaks the word to end the drought.

In a region of the world where it is in short supply, water naturally features prominently in the lives of the people of the Bible. Nothing is more life-threatening than the absence of water; nothing more life-giving than rain. It becomes a symbol of God's favour and goodness, and of thirst-quenching spiritual refreshment. In Christ, the living water and water of life, it is linked to everlasting life as the supreme blessing that God gives.

God of rain, we thank you for our water, plentiful and unpolluted;
we thank you for Jesus, a spring of water gushing up to eternal life. Amen

TIM HEATON

Summer sounds

Praise the Lord! Praise the Lord from the heavens; praise him in the heights! Praise him, all his angels; praise him, all his host! Praise him, sun and moon; praise him, all you shining stars! Praise him, you highest heavens, and you waters above the heavens! Let them praise the name of the Lord, for he commanded and they were created. He established them forever and ever; he fixed their bounds, which cannot be passed. Praise the Lord from the earth, you sea monsters and all deeps, fire and hail, snow and frost, stormy wind fulfilling his command! Mountains and all hills, fruit trees and all cedars! Wild animals and all cattle, creeping things and flying birds!

The birdsong has mostly stopped now: it is too hot and the birds cannot be bothered to sing any more. But all around there is a new noise, a low insectile drone, the constant hum and buzz of bees and other flying insects. The meadow grasshopper is also making its sound by rubbing its wings against its legs. This is high summer, and you can hear the full sound of nature.

The 'creeping things' (v. 10) are praising God, joining their speech and sounds to the voice of all creation. Psalm 148 must have inspired the Benedicite (Song of the Three Children), one of the Prayer Book canticles of Morning Prayer: 'O all ye works of the Lord, bless ye the Lord: praise him, and magnify him forever.' In the Old Testament the root meanings of the various words used for 'praise' are connected with either making a noise, bodily gestures or the playing and singing of music.

There are other sounds of summer too: lawnmowers, strimmers and hedge cutters; outdoor events and celebrations. Over the noise of the world there rises a melody, the hymn of praise of every created thing giving glory to God their creator. As Isaiah put it, 'The mountains and the hills before you shall burst into song, and all the trees of the field shall clap their hands' (Isaiah 55:12). If we were silent, even the stones would shout out (Luke 19:40).

God of all creation, of sun and moon, mountains and trees, wild animals and creeping things, we raise to you with them our sacrifice of praise. Amen

TIM HEATON

Summer smells

Just after daybreak, Jesus stood on the beach; but the disciples did not know that it was Jesus… When they had gone ashore, they saw a charcoal fire there, with fish on it, and bread. Jesus said to them, 'Bring some of the fish that you have just caught.' So Simon Peter went aboard and hauled the net ashore, full of large fish, a hundred and fifty-three of them; and though there were so many, the net was not torn. Jesus said to them, 'Come and have breakfast.' Now none of the disciples dared to ask him, 'Who are you?' because they knew it was the Lord.

The aroma of chargrilled food wafts on a warm breeze from a neighbour's garden. It is one of many wonderful smells of summer: the fragrance of freshly mown grass; the heavenly scent of roses, lavender or honeysuckle. Other people and places may instantly be recalled. Scent is a powerful memory trigger: the olfactory nerve, which is responsible for our sense of smell, is located close to the hippocampus, the part of the brain that converts data into long-term memories.

John the Evangelist writes his account of the barbecue on the beach as an eyewitness. He was there, the disciple whom Jesus loved. He would have remembered another day in Galilee when Jesus fed the multitude with the same food: fish and bread. The early church saw eucharistic symbolism in that miracle of the multiplication of loaves and fishes, and Jesus' preparation of this simple meal on the seashore for his friends confirms him as both the bestower of kindness and the source of life-sustaining nourishment.

Once more the host becomes the Host: 'Please, have some bread; this is my body, broken for you.' The meal confirms the intimacy of the relationship between the risen Lord and his disciples; indeed it is the meal that becomes the moment of recognition, just as it did at Emmaus (Luke 24:13–31). There is fellowship, hospitality and the desire to serve others. Perhaps you might think about inviting some friends for a meal one day if you can. You could be as Christ to them.

Great God and giver of all good things, may we remember your love each time we eat and when we share our food with others. Amen

TIM HEATON

Hotter summers

The seven years of plenty that prevailed in the land of Egypt came to an end; and the seven years of famine began to come, just as Joseph had said. There was famine in every country, but throughout the land of Egypt there was bread. When all the land of Egypt was famished, the people cried to Pharaoh for bread. Pharaoh said to all the Egyptians, 'Go to Joseph; what he says to you, do.' And since the famine had spread over all the land, Joseph opened all the storehouses, and sold to the Egyptians, for the famine was severe in the land of Egypt. Moreover, all the world came to Joseph in Egypt to buy grain, because the famine became severe throughout the world.

A report from Oxfam in 2021 said that eleven people in the world were dying of hunger every minute. More than 150 million were living in crisis levels of food insecurity, with climate change and the Covid pandemic pushing food prices to new highs. The worst hunger spots were war-torn countries, including Afghanistan, South Sudan, Syria and Yemen, but there is no doubt that global warming is becoming a deadly contributor to severe food shortage.

In the characteristic biblical doctrine of divine providence, Egypt's seven years of plenty and seven years of famine were of God's doing (Genesis 41:25, 32); God, who controls the forces of nature, can withdraw the fruits of nature, presumably in this instance to bring Joseph's brothers to Egypt. Today we accept that our actions have consequences, including the way we have mistreated our planet. We also acknowledge the terrible injustice of climate change, which is that among the nations suffering most from its effects are those that have caused it the least.

It is hardly newsworthy any more that global heat records are being broken annually, causing natural disasters. Droughts, heatwaves, fires and floods are all killer events in their own right – not just for humans, but also for many animals – but climate change is also making it even harder to feed the world. The injustice must be ended.

God of our ancestors, of Abraham, Isaac and Jacob, in your goodness feed the hungry, and bless the work of aid agencies working for famine relief. Amen

TIM HEATON

Another summer

Then Noah built an altar to the Lord, and took of every clean animal and of every clean bird, and offered burnt-offerings on the altar. And when the Lord smelt the pleasing odour, the Lord said in his heart, 'I will never again curse the ground because of humankind, for the inclination of the human heart is evil from youth; nor will I ever again destroy every living creature as I have done. As long as the earth endures, seedtime and harvest, cold and heat, summer and winter, day and night, shall not cease.'

Summer is not over yet but one day it will be. The changing of the seasons is part of the rhythm of the natural world that keeps time with the beat of the universe. Summer will pass into autumn as surely as the leafing of the fig tree signalled that summer was near. The days will become cooler and the leaves on the trees will start to change colour. Around 23 September, the autumnal equinox, the sun, continuing its apparent motion from north to south, will cross the equator to bless other climes and summer here will be gone.

Autumn will bring joys of its own, but there is an inevitable sadness in the passing of summer. Those who suffer from seasonal affective disorder, sometimes known as 'winter depression', will feel it more than others. But for most of us, as we return to work and education, there is a sense that something has gone, something good and beautiful, something heavenly. There will be special memories of people and places, extended leisure time and holidays.

But God has promised another summer: summer and winter shall not cease (v. 22). After the flood, God's resolve is not to destroy but to save and renew, and the rainbow in the sky is the sign of that covenant. As we end this series of reflections, we might take with us the thought that faith is not just *believing in God* but *trusting in the promises of God*. God has spoken; it will be so. There will be another summer.

Faithful God, whose promises never fail, make us worthy to be called your followers, trusting and obedient, and ready to serve you to the end. Amen

TIM HEATON

The road to Jerusalem

 Do you enjoy travelling? I do, whether by car or train, boat or plane. To me a journey is a challenge as well as an enjoyable experience. Many things can happen on a journey, and we must adapt and adjust as we go along until at last we safely reach our destination.

For the next two weeks our attention will be on Luke 17—20, a section of his gospel that describes the final journey of Jesus to Jerusalem and the last days of his life. In these action-packed chapters, we are invited to follow Jesus as he makes his way ever nearer to the city and his eventual death.

This is a period of rich teaching with many parables and much instruction about the kingdom of God. The journey is full of incident and involves significant interactions with individuals. We meet the ten lepers, parents with their children, a blind beggar, a wealthy ruler and the crafty tax collector called Zacchaeus. It is always worth taking time to see how Jesus deals with people, sensitive to each one, seeking only to help them to grow more fully into the life of the kingdom and yield to the rule of God.

We also see Jesus in dialogue with the religious leaders of the city, skilfully answering their tricky questions yet still incurring their wrath. Scripture is fulfilled before our eyes when he enters triumphantly into Jerusalem, only then to be rejected. We look on aghast as the plot against him gains momentum, fuelled by jealousy and a stubborn refusal to believe. Not everyone is willing to receive the kingdom or recognise the king.

The journey on foot takes us from Galilee and the border of Samaria, past Jericho and on to Bethany and Bethpage, then down the road to the Mount of Olives. We watch, we listen and hopefully we learn as he reaches the city and begins to teach in the temple.

Why not make your own journey with Jesus by opening yourself to Luke's telling of the story. No dusty road for you to travel, only a sanctified use of your imagination to help you enter into these holy moments and the prayer that you may follow faithfully in his footsteps as you also choose to do the Father's will.

TONY HORSFALL

Watch yourselves

Jesus said to his disciples: 'Things that cause people to stumble are bound to come, but woe to anyone through whom they come. It would be better for them to be thrown into the sea with a millstone tied round their neck than to cause one of these little ones to stumble. So watch yourselves. If your brother or sister sins against you, rebuke them; and if they repent, forgive them. Even if they sin against you seven times in a day and seven times come back to you saying "I repent," you must forgive them.'

Relationships are often tricky, aren't they? In the context of the church, we expect to be able to get on well with everyone, but for some reason this is never straightforward. We upset each other, say things that wound and sometimes behave unkindly. We get hurt, and we hurt others.

Jesus, ever the realist when it comes to human nature, asks his followers to watch themselves, to take care of their relationships. With typical eastern hyperbole, he warns us against being the cause of damage in the lives of others, especially those who are younger in years or less mature in their faith. Here he sets out a little formula for mending broken relationships.

First, nip things in the bud. If someone hurts you in some way, speak to them directly about it. This is far healthier than gossiping to another person or allowing it to fester inside you.

Second, when a person apologises or says sorry, readily forgive them and lay the matter to rest. Refuse to hold grudges or to keep harping on about it. To forgive is to release a person from their mistake and to restore the relationship back to normal.

Finally, even if someone repeats their mistake frequently, our responsibility is to keep on forgiving, which is never easy. Even the apostle Peter struggled with this. But to harbour a lack of forgiveness will be more damaging.

When a friend told me I had behaved in a patronising way towards her, I was shocked, but I realised I needed to ask her forgiveness. I did, and the relationship was restored. Do you need to either give or receive forgiveness? How might you need to 'watch yourself' when it comes to your relationships?

TONY HORSFALL

Gratitude to God

As he was going into a village, ten men who had leprosy met him. They stood at a distance and called out in a loud voice, 'Jesus, Master, have pity on us!' When he saw them, he said, 'Go, show yourselves to the priests.' And as they went, they were cleansed. One of them, when he saw he was healed, came back, praising God in a loud voice. He threw himself at Jesus' feet and thanked him – and he was a Samaritan. Jesus asked, 'Were not all ten cleansed? Where are the other nine? Has no one returned to give praise to God except this foreigner?' Then he said to him, 'Rise and go; your faith has made you well.'

Leprosy was a crippling disease, disfiguring those who caught it, and isolating them from society. Lepers felt rejected, spiritually inferior and socially outcast. The ten lepers whom Jesus met on the road must have banded together for friendship, mutual support and safety. A shared need often brings people closer together. The compassionate Christ responded to their cry for mercy. As they went by faith to show themselves to the priest, each one was healed. What joy they must have felt.

Jesus is amazed that only one returned to give thanks to God, and a despised Samaritan at that. How easy it is to ask God to do things for us, and then when he does, to forget to acknowledge his goodness. We pray, but when our prayers are answered, we do not always spend time in thanksgiving. Nor do we always share our testimony to the goodness of God.

The practice of gratitude is more than a polite cultural response to kindness, it is a spiritual discipline. Indeed, we can choose to find reasons every day to be grateful. A friend of mine, for example, closes her day by noting down three things for which she can give thanks. Such an attitude and approach to life will make us happier and more positive in our outlook. It is good for our mental health and emotional well-being. Rather than grumbling and complaining, we can choose to identify the good things that God has done and give thanks accordingly.

For what are you grateful? Is there someone whom you want to thank?
Are you daily expressing your gratitude to God?

TONY HORSFALL

The coming king

Once, on being asked by the Pharisees when the kingdom of God would come, Jesus replied, 'The coming of the kingdom of God is not something that can be observed, nor will people say, "Here it is," or "There it is," because the kingdom of God is in your midst. Then he said to his disciples, 'The time is coming when you will long to see one of the days of the Son of Man, but you will not see it. People will tell you, "There he is!" or "Here he is!" Do not go running off after them. For the Son of Man in his day will be like the lightning, which flashes and lights up the sky from one end to the other. But first he must suffer many things and be rejected by this generation.'

In the psyche of the people of Israel was a longing to see God break into the world and demonstrate his power and justice, to show that he was in control. In particular, they wanted to see their enemies defeated and their land liberated. Jesus spoke often about the kingdom of God, but in a different sense.

For Jesus, the kingdom is the realm where God's rule is recognised and welcomed. It was not political in nature, but spiritual, and this was the message he came to proclaim: 'The kingdom of God has come near' (Mark 1:15).

In explaining this concept to the Pharisees, Jesus says there is no need to look elsewhere for the kingdom of God, it is already present because he is there, in their midst. Jesus is the embodiment of the rule of God, perfectly displaying what it means to live to do God's will. The kingdom of God is within.

In explaining this to his disciples, he hints that he will one day return in the full glory of that kingdom, but they will not see it because it is in the future. What they will see is something that will appear to contradict the idea that he is king – they will see him crucified and put to death. This king is one who must first suffer to open the way for others to enter the kingdom.

Lord, help me to understand the true nature of the kingdom. Amen

TONY HORSFALL

Be ready

'Just as it was in the days of Noah, so also will it be in the days of the Son of Man. People were eating, drinking, marrying and being given in marriage up to the day Noah entered the ark. Then the flood came and destroyed them all. It was the same in the days of Lot. People were eating and drinking, buying and selling, planting and building. But the day Lot left Sodom, fire and sulphur rained down from heaven and destroyed them all. It will be just like this on the day the Son of Man is revealed.'

For most people life follows a familiar pattern and routine. Even when society is collapsing and evil abounds, things seem to go on as normal. When it is business as usual, we may not realise the danger we are in.

Noah lived at such a time when wickedness had increased to the extent that God decided to start again, and the earth was flooded. Lot likewise lived in a city that was so perverted even the intercession of Abraham could make no difference and it experienced a cataclysmic destruction.

The idea of the judgement of God is unpalatable to modern ears, but it is impossible to read the story of Israel without seeing that sin has consequences and that evil cannot be allowed to take over. Sooner or later, God will act to stem the tide of wickedness.

God's wrath (his response to evil) is never without mercy, however. In Noah's day escape was provided by the building of an ark. For Lot and his family, salvation came through two angelic visitors who led them to a place of safety. There is always a way of escape for those who seek it and who are willing to turn from evil. Both stories point to the salvation that is available to us through Jesus.

We also live in times where evil is rampant. There has been a wholesale rejection of God's laws in our day. Wherever we look, evil abounds yet we must not be lulled into any false sense of security by the normality of life. We must find a place of refuge for ourselves, and do so at once, before it is too late. We will not be turned away.

Lord, help me to be ready and alert in the face of evil. Amen

TONY HORSFALL

Persevering in prayer

Then Jesus told his disciples a parable to show them that they should always pray and not give up. He said: 'In a certain town there was a judge who neither feared God nor cared for what people thought. And there was a widow in that town who kept coming to him with the plea, "Grant me justice against my adversary." For some time he refused. But finally he said to himself, "Even though I don't fear God or care what people think, yet because this widow keeps bothering me, I will see that she gets justice, so that she won't eventually come and attack me!"' And the Lord said, 'Listen to what the unjust judge says. And will not God bring about justice for his chosen ones, who cry out to him day and night?'

This parable reminds me of the story of the 32-year campaign for justice by the families of those killed in the Hillsborough Stadium disaster of 1989, a story of persistence and fighting against the odds. Mostly people from poorer backgrounds, the group had to take on the self-protective culture of the establishment, but in the end, they won their case.

The key lesson here is that God is not like the judge in the story. He is neither unjust nor reluctant to help. God is always responsive to our prayer, but the very nature of prayer requires that we must persist in our praying. If prayer were always answered instantaneously, we would never learn to appreciate the goodness of God. Praying is not like rubbing a magic lamp. When answers to our prayers are delayed, we must dig deep within ourselves and find the grit and determination to persist. In this way our character is being shaped and our trust in God increased.

Further, in this life justice may be slow to come and we will need to set our hope on Jesus, and in particular the promise of his return when all wrongs will be righted. We will need to keep believing and trusting until the day of his coming again.

Am I willing to persist in my prayer, and not give up? Can I continue to trust that my cry for justice will be heard? God loves such steely determination in his children.

TONY HORSFALL

Humble before God

To some who were confident of their own righteousness and looked down on everyone else, Jesus told this parable: 'Two men went up to the temple to pray, one a Pharisee and the other a tax collector. The Pharisee stood by himself and prayed, "God, I thank you that I am not like other people – robbers, evildoers, adulterers – or even like this tax collector. I fast twice a week and give a tenth of all I get." But the tax collector stood at a distance. He would not even look up to heaven, but beat his breast and said, "God, have mercy on me, a sinner."'

The great danger of a rules-based approach to Christianity is that if you manage to do everything right you end up feeling proud, but if you fail you are left feeling miserable.

The Pharisee in this parable represents all those who successfully strive to keep the rules (as they see them) and find that they have developed an inflated sense of their own goodness and with it a superior attitude towards lesser mortals. Their confidence lies in their own performance and self-righteousness, which they deem to be acceptable to God. To their surprise they discover that God is not impressed by their achievements.

The tax collector, on the other hand, represents those who have failed (often repeatedly and spectacularly) in their attempts to be good, and instead cast themselves on the mercy of God. They can put no confidence in their own performance but stand in need of grace. To their surprise they discover that they are accepted by a God who loves to show mercy to the needy and who is not put off by human failure.

Jesus is making this point: if we exalt ourselves, we will be humbled; but if we humble ourselves, we will be exalted (Luke 18:14). If we think we have lived perfectly, then we have deceived ourselves, and can never know the joy of receiving grace. If we know we have failed, and are willing to admit it, we stand open to receive the wonder of God's forgiveness and acceptance.

Am I trusting in my own efforts to be right with God or depending on his grace?

Lord, help me to approach you in the humility of my need,
not the complacency of my pride. Amen

TONY HORSFALL

Become like little children

People were also bringing babies to Jesus for him to place his hands on them. When the disciples saw this, they rebuked them. But Jesus called the children to him and said, 'Let the little children come to me, and do not hinder them, for the kingdom of God belongs to such as these. Truly I tell you, anyone who will not receive the kingdom of God like a little child will never enter it.'

From my childhood in Sunday School, I have a strong memory of the Cradle Roll, a picture of Jesus as the good shepherd, with children gathered around him and spaces to write in the names of those who had been baptised. It spoke to me then about a Saviour who welcomes and accepts children. Yet how easy it is to undervalue their place in the church; little ones can be seen as an inconvenience and a disturbance, to be tolerated rather than loved, to be put up with rather than treasured for who they are.

Jesus is very clear that children belong in the kingdom of God. They are to be included and given value and significance within the Christian community. This means that those who work with children, whether in Sunday school, Messy Church, kids' clubs, toddler groups, youth groups and so on, are to be celebrated and honoured, for they are doing kingdom work of the highest order. Consequently, the work they do has to be well resourced and publicly recognised.

Notice here how Jesus is willing to bless the babies, laying his hands upon them to communicate the love of God to them in their earliest days, and how he calls the older children to be with him and to learn to be his followers too.

There is, however, a sting in the tail – a challenge to the adults. We cannot enter the kingdom unless we become child-like, that is, adopting a humble attitude and a simplicity of faith that trusts God and takes him at his word. Grown-ups sometimes have a danger of being too sophisticated, too clever for their own good, which makes progress in God's humble kingdom difficult.

What is my attitude towards the children in my church?
What does it mean to be child-like in faith?

TONY HORSFALL

Riches and the kingdom

A certain ruler asked him, 'Good teacher, what must I do to inherit eternal life?' 'Why do you call me good?' Jesus answered. 'No one is good – except God alone. You know the commandments: "You shall not commit adultery, you shall not murder, you shall not steal, you shall not give false testimony, honour your father and mother."' 'All these I have kept since I was a boy,' he said. When Jesus heard this, he said to him, 'You still lack one thing. Sell everything you have and give to the poor, and you will have treasure in heaven. Then come, follow me.' When he heard this, he became very sad, because he was very wealthy. Jesus looked at him and said, 'How hard it is for the rich to enter the kingdom of God! Indeed, it is easier for a camel to go through the eye of a needle than for someone who is rich to enter the kingdom of God.'

A wealthy man was once asked the question, 'How much money is enough?' He replied honestly, 'Just a little more.' Money plays a big part in anyone's life. This young man came to Jesus sincerely desiring a spiritual life. From childhood he had carefully kept the commandments, seeking to win God's approval, living a good life in every way. Yet he was blind to the grip that his wealth had upon his soul. Jesus, the physician of souls, immediately diagnosed his problem and asked him to free himself from its grip by giving to the poor. The man's sorrowful refusal revealed that money was more important to him than God.

Why is wealth such a drawback to kingdom living? Because it can make us feel self-sufficient and secure within ourselves. Acquiring wealth often demands long hours at work and creates the attendant sins of greed and materialism. A simple lifestyle is far more conducive to spiritual growth. Yet generosity of heart is characteristic of God and therefore of the citizens of his kingdom. Money can be used well to expand and resource the work of God, and to support those called to ministry, but this always requires the willingness to give it away.

What is your attitude towards money? How generous are you? How might you bless others by sharing your resources with them?

TONY HORSFALL

Ready to die

Jesus took the Twelve aside and told them, 'We are going up to Jerusalem, and everything that is written by the prophets about the Son of Man will be fulfilled. He will be handed over to the Gentiles. They will mock him, insult him and spit on him; they will flog him and kill him. On the third day he will rise again.' The disciples did not understand any of this. Its meaning was hidden from them, and they did not know what he was talking about.

Have you ever faced major surgery, or painful dental treatment? Most of us recoil at the thought and meet it with a sense of dread. We would all rather avoid suffering and prefer not to be speak about it.

I love the way that Jesus takes the twelve disciples aside to talk with them privately. He has some important and disturbing things to share with them, and this is better done in person, away from the crowds. His careful handling of the disciples is a feature of the gospel story. He is continually nurturing their faith, expanding their minds and forming their character.

There is no sense of denial here as Jesus thinks about his future. He is under no illusions about the fate that awaits him as he bravely goes up to Jerusalem. This will be a journey with no return. He is going there to die.

Neither is there anything fatalistic in his thinking. He is conscious that as the Son of Man he will face suffering, for this is clearly foretold in the scriptures. He knows his death will be an essential part of the whole plan of salvation, and so he willingly embraces it. It will involve hostility and cruel treatment, yet he courageously steps forward to embrace the Father's will for him. He can do this because he knows he will rise again.

The disciples are flummoxed. They cannot yet imagine their friend dying or conceive of a suffering Messiah. They are in denial, still hoping for a political deliverer. They have yet to grasp the essential nature of the kingdom as being spiritual, not political. The kingdom comes not by force but by sacrifice.

Consider: 'It is the way the master went; should not the servant tread it still?' (Horatius Bonar, 1808–89).

TONY HORSFALL

A pertinent question

As Jesus approached Jericho, a blind man was sitting by the roadside begging. When he heard the crowd going by, he asked what was happening. They told him, 'Jesus of Nazareth is passing by.' He called out, 'Jesus, Son of David, have mercy on me!' Those who led the way rebuked him and told him to be quiet, but he shouted all the more, 'Son of David, have mercy of me!' Jesus stopped and ordered the man to be brought to him. When he came near, Jesus asked him, 'What do you want me to do for you?' 'Lord, I want to see,' he replied. Jesus said to him, 'Receive your sight; your faith has healed you.' Immediately he received his sight and followed Jesus, praising God.

Do you ever find yourself preoccupied? I find that when I am preoccupied with my troubles or focused on my work, I am not always so aware of the needs of those around me, not just strangers, but sometimes even family and friends.

Despite thoughts of his coming death crowding his mind, Jesus is not so preoccupied with his own concerns that he cannot hear a cry for help or find time to stop and respond to the man's plea. This was no influential person who might warrant special treatment, but a poor blind beggar whose daily occupation was to sit by the roadside and hope passers-by would have pity on him. He sat at the bottom of the social scale, and those leading the way for Jesus assume that the master will not have time for such a lowly person. How wrong they are!

Jesus stops to listen and attend to the man, and asks pertinently, 'What do you want me to do for you?' (v. 41). It is a moment of opportunity which the man grasps with both hands. It is also a question which lies at the heart of the spiritual life, and one we should ponder. Perhaps you have been crying out in your need. Tell Jesus exactly what it is you want him to do for you. What is your deepest desire? What is your most earnest longing? Don't make a surface response but look deeper inside yourself. Jesus is aware of you. You have his full attention.

Jesus, you know my needs and desires, and those of others.
Hear our prayers. Amen

TONY HORSFALL

Loosening the purse strings

When Jesus reached the spot, he looked up and said to him, 'Zacchaeus, come down immediately. I must stay at your house today.' So he came down at once and welcomed him gladly. All the people saw this and began to mutter, 'He has gone to be the guest of a sinner.' But Zacchaeus stood up and said to the Lord, 'Look, Lord! Here and now I give half of my possessions to the poor, and if I have cheated anybody out of anything, I will pay back four times the amount.' Jesus said to him, 'Today salvation has come to this house, because this man, too, is a son of Abraham. For the Son of Man came to seek and to save the lost.'

The famous missionary and writer Amy Carmichael said, 'You can give without love, but you cannot love without giving.' In great contrast to the story of the rich ruler (Luke 18:18–30; see Sunday 30 July), here a wealthy man loosens his purse strings to bless the poor and make restitution to those he has cheated: a sure sign that the kingdom has come to his heart.

Once again Jesus, free from self-preoccupation, notices someone in need. Alert to what God is doing, he sees Zacchaeus, a despised tax collector, perched high in the tree, and invites himself to his home. This public recognition of a well-known scoundrel was a declaration that the kingdom is open to all who sincerely seek God. Jesus is happy to keep company with sinners.

In responding to the call of Jesus, and opening his home and his heart, Zacchaeus receives the gift of salvation. True salvation not only means the forgiveness of our sins but also a change of life. The genuineness of Zacchaeus' response is evidenced in his sadness at how he has behaved and his willingness to make amends. The shackles of the love of money have been broken and he is free to live a life of generosity. It is always good to ask yourself, 'How has my salvation impacted my life? What changes am I making as I follow Jesus?'

Jesus often chooses the unlikeliest and least deserving of people to be his followers. He comes for the broken, the needy, the despised and the rejected. His love has no limits.

TONY HORSFALL

The king is here!

As they were untying the colt, its owners asked them, 'Why are you untying the colt?' They replied, 'The Lord needs it.' They brought it to Jesus, put their cloaks on the colt and put Jesus on it. As he went along, people spread their cloaks on the road. When he came near the place where the road goes down the Mount of Olives, the whole crowd of disciples began joyfully to praise God in loud voices for all the miracles they had seen: 'Blessed is the king who comes in the name of the Lord!' 'Peace in heaven and glory in the highest!' Some of the Pharisees in the crowd said to Jesus, 'Teacher, rebuke your disciples!' 'I tell you,' he replied, 'if they keep quiet, the stones will cry out.'

Whereas victorious Roman generals would enter Rome on a white stallion, with much pomp and ceremony, Jesus enters Jerusalem in a humbler way. There is no doubt that he was aware of the statement he was making as he rode into the city on a lowly donkey. Not only was this a fulfilment of Psalm 118:26, but also Zechariah 9:9 (as Matthew records, 21:5). Jesus was saying, 'I am the one of whom the prophets spoke, the humble king who will establish the kingdom of God.

As we have seen already, for most Jews, belief in the coming of a king developed into an idea of a political figure who would overthrow the Romans and liberate them from their enemies. The miracles they saw fuelled the fire of expectation, but Jesus is thinking in an altogether different way. He knows that he is called to be a suffering servant, that his kingdom will be based on peace not war, and lowliness not pride. He was going to Jerusalem to die, to usher in the kingdom of God not by violence and the sword but through love and sacrifice.

There is great excitement as he enters Jerusalem. Jesus is worthy of the highest praise, especially when we understand his death and the nature of the kingdom. And it remains true that if we fail to praise him, the very stones will do so. Let us not hold back in our celebrations of the king or be frugal in our worship.

Jesus enters Jerusalem humbly, revealing a different and new way of thinking about kingship. How do you see kingship today?

TONY HORSFALL

A spy story

The teachers of the law and the chief priests looked for a way to arrest him immediately, because they knew he had spoken this parable against them. But they were afraid of the people. Keeping a close watch on him, they sent spies, who pretended to be sincere. They hoped to catch Jesus in something he said, so that they might hand him over to the power and authority of the governor. So the spies questioned him: 'Teacher, we know that you speak and teach what is right, and that you do not show partiality but teach the way of God in accordance with the truth. Is it right for us to pay taxes to Caesar or not?'

Espionage and subterfuge do not belong exclusively to modern times. Jesus now is not only in Jerusalem but teaching regularly in the temple courts. The hostility against him from the religious authorities is now at boiling point, and they are looking for a way to arrest him, hence the planting of the spies. They would have been bolder in their scheming were it not for the fact that Jesus was so popular.

Their strategy is clear. They want to catch Jesus out with a trick question and get him to say something to incriminate himself. Like a shrewd and devious media interviewer they ask about paying taxes to Caesar. It is a thorny question: if he says 'Yes', he will outrage the Jewish nationalists; if he if says 'No', he will be in trouble with the Romans. No doubt they are very pleased with this dilemma.

Jesus, however, outsmarts them by taking a Roman coin bearing Caesar's image and inscription and giving the advice, 'Give back to Caesar what is Caesar's, and to God what is God's' (Luke 20:25). Here is a guiding principle of good citizenship. Yes, we must obey the ruling authorities and pay taxes, a teaching elucidated by the apostle Paul (Romans 13:1–7). Yet the highest authority is God's, and we must submit to his rule. Only if there is a specific clash are we to obey God rather than earthly rulers (Acts 5:29).

Jesus was not deceived by their duplicity, nor is he fooled by our insincerity. He knows the human heart, and only the genuine and sincere can live in harmony with him.

TONY HORSFALL

The temptations of power

While all the people were listening, Jesus said to his disciples, 'Beware of the teachers of the law. They like to walk around in flowing robes and love to be greeted with respect in the market-places and have the most important seats in the synagogues and the places of honour at banquets. They devour widows' houses and for a show make lengthy prayers. These men will be punished most severely.'

I read that the late Archbishop Desmond Tutu made a habit while travelling abroad of always making his own bed, even in hotels. He would explain to the staff that he was not dissatisfied with their work, but it was his way of keeping himself grounded and not being carried away by either popularity or fame. As the servant of a humble king, I am sure his master would have approved.

Jesus was never afraid to challenge the religious leaders of his day or expose their faults to his disciples lest they should imitate a wrong model of leadership. He set an example of humility and integrity which he expects us to imitate. Servant leadership is not weak leadership.

It is a prime temptation among leaders to get carried away by their status and to love the praise of other people. Even within the church there can be a celebrity culture, and while we should honour our leaders and those who preach God's word, we do them no favours by putting them on a pedestal.

Jesus is clear that leaders should not use their position of influence for personal gain or to take advantage of those who put their trust in them. Neither should they like the sound of their own voice or be carried away by their own eloquence, especially in prayer.

Those who find themselves in the spotlight and whose giftedness endears them to people should remember who they serve and seek to live and minister with humility. They must be aware of the subtle dangers inherent in prominence and power, and the corrosive effect adulation can have on their own spiritual lives. Leaders will be judged with greater strictness. Of those to whom much is given, much will be required (Luke 12:48).

Lord, thank you for good leaders. May we always encourage them but without flattery, remembering that they too are human.

TONY HORSFALL

The temple

 While my birth family was Hindu, we did not partake in temple worship, although I have visited several temples. The key is knowing whose temple, since each is the earthly dwelling of a particular god. (The film *Indiana Jones and the Temple of Doom* offers fascinating insights on 20th-century western ideas about ancient temples.) Meanwhile, I wonder how many people who declare, 'My body is a temple,' know they are misquoting the Bible and realise what they are saying about themselves. Alongside the concept of temples being grand and beautiful, perhaps the statement betrays a desire to be an object of worship. Left to our own devices, most of us place ourselves at the centre of the universe. Maybe this is one reason for Christians to rediscover what the Bible says about God and the temple.

All of us probably have some notion of the temple in Jerusalem, and there are likely to be as many ways of approaching a series of studies on this as there are references in the Bible. Over the next couple of weeks, I invite you to explore the story of the temple: its history and its centrality to Jesus and New Testament writers and thereby to us. As a result, I shall not focus on details of the physical building, the role of priests and others, the sacrifices, nor on much else which is fascinating about the temple. Do continue your own reading and research into these aspects.

Instead, these studies will offer snapshots, beginning with the way God initially allowed a physical symbol of divine presence among God's people in the wilderness. Examination of who built the temple, where and why, might cause us to wonder and worship. The subsequent destruction and rebuilding of the temple offer opportunities for reflection on the human condition and perhaps lament, as well as hope in God's mercy. Jesus revolutionised and fulfilled everything about the temple. Now Christians experience the Holy Spirit in God's world without kingdom hope fully realised. We have instructions about the nature of the temple and a vision of heaven to help us to live as God's people. My prayer for you as you study these passages, is to grasp more fully your place in God's story and God's presence with you.

LAKSHMI JEFFREYS

A holy dwelling

The Lord said to Moses, 'Tell the Israelites to make an offering to me. Receive whatever offerings anyone wishes to give. These offerings are to be: gold, silver, and bronze; fine linen; blue, purple, and red wool; cloth made of goats' hair; rams' skin dyed red; fine leather; acacia wood; oil for the lamps; spices for the anointing oil and for the sweet-smelling incense; carnelians and other jewels to be set in the ephod of the High Priest and in his breastpiece. The people must make a sacred Tent for me, so that I may live among them.'

God would reside among God's people. Think about what that means. While it is not unusual for nomadic tribes, even today, to have a special tent containing idols in the middle of their camp, Yahweh, the God of heaven, the God whose name was so holy it could not be spoken, was different. The people had been expressly forbidden to make idols, yet their God would inhabit a tent among them. And this would be no ordinary tent! (It is worth reading the incredible details of the measurements, the materials to be used and the care with which the tabernacle was constructed.)

As God's people were being formed, God was holy, distant, other, only to be approached in certain ways by specific people on designated occasions. At the same time, there was a sign of this God in the middle of the (relatively) tiny group of refugees, so that dwellers in the settlements around the desert might see and wonder. God remained in heaven and at the same time was present among the people, travelling with them and leading them to the promised land.

The glory of the infinite 'I Am' was housed in a tabernacle, constructed as a result of free-will offerings. This God now shines in our hearts to reveal the light of the knowledge of the glory of God in the face of Jesus Christ (2 Corinthians 4:6). It is relatively easy to give money or goods towards something physical, intended to reveal God's glory in the world. What might God ask you to offer that is less tangible?

Holy God, abiding with us, may we give as you ask, that those around may see your glory. Amen

LAKSHMI JEFFREYS

Costly sacrifice

'Take it, my lord the king, and use it as you wish,' Araunah said to David. 'Here are oxen for the burnt offering, and you can use the threshing boards and ox yokes for wood to build a fire on the altar. I will give it all to you, Your Majesty, and may the Lord your God accept your sacrifice.' But the king replied to Araunah, 'No, I insist on buying it, for I will not present burnt offerings to the Lord my God that have cost me nothing.' So David paid him fifty pieces of silver for the threshing floor and the oxen.

The site of the temple in Jerusalem had form! Abraham had been told to sacrifice Isaac here. God's angel of death was standing on the threshing floor, ready to destroy Jerusalem, until God instructed the angel to stop. (Read the whole chapter to discover what David had done to incur God's wrath.) Desperate to save his people and atone for his sin, David begs to know what he should do and is told to build an altar. Although Araunah is willing to give David whatever he wants, the king recognises that sacrifice is costly. David's son, Solomon would eventually build the temple in this very place and priests would sacrifice burnt offerings as prescribed by the law. Finally, this area of Jerusalem would be known as Calvary, the location of the costliest sacrifice ever.

Yesterday we touched on the cost of constructing the tabernacle through free-will offerings from the people. Today the emphasis is not on generosity but on sacrifice, although the two are often linked. At the time of writing, there is news of people facing economic hardship, sacrificing warm surroundings in order to afford food for the household. Such sacrifices feel not so much generous as necessary. Temple sacrifice, on the other hand, was to thank God, atone for sin or to ask God for something. There was a sacrifice for every aspect of life.

What do we sacrifice today, when we praise and thank God, confess sin or petition God or intercede? Of course, Jesus' sacrifice on the cross means there is no need for a formal sacrificial system. Perhaps God asks us to sacrifice pride or self-will.

'The sacrifice acceptable to God is a broken spirit; a broken and contrite heart, O God, you will not despise' (Psalm 51:17, NRSV).

LAKSHMI JEFFREYS

Rest and responsibility

David said, 'The Lord, the God of Israel, has given us peace, and he will always live in Jerusalem. Now the Levites will no longer need to carry the Tabernacle and its furnishings from place to place.' In accordance with David's final instructions, all the Levites twenty years old or older were registered for service... And so, under the supervision of the priests, the Levites watched over the Tabernacle and the Temple and faithfully carried out their duties of service at the house of the Lord.

This passage has a personal resonance: our church building is undergoing repairs, so we have been camping out in a school and other buildings, kindly offered by groups within the community. Having to carry various items from edifice to another for different acts of worship has often resulted in choosing between doing without whatever we have forgotten or starting the service late. It will be wonderful when everything is in one place and people can resume their normal duties, rather than adding 'porter' to the list!

Peace – shalom – is the sense of complete well-being, promised by God when the people live God's way. The tabernacle had been replaced by the temple. The people were settled in one place and God would settle with them. There would be the requirement for sacrifices and rituals, but these would be part of daily life. The Levites were relieved of porter duties and could focus on daily worship of God.

Place and peace are significant themes in the Bible. Jesus did miracles in places that had known tragedy. In 1996, the Scottish town of Dunblane hit the headlines when a gunman killed 16 young children and their teacher in the local school. The subsequent Snowdrop Campaign, initiated by families in the town, resulted in tighter gun laws in the UK. More recently, in response to overwhelming knife crime, *The Knife Angel* was sculpted from 100,000 knives, seized during knife amnesties across the UK.

God's presence brings peace. An immediate challenge for our church is to discern that peace while moving from one location to another. The task more widely for Christians is to discover how to be peacemakers wherever we are.

Pray for and learn about the Snowdrop Campaign, The Knife Angel and other projects, seeking to bring peace to areas of conflict.

LAKSHMI JEFFREYS

Temple constructed

Now the word of the Lord came to Solomon, 'Concerning this house that you are building, if you will walk in my statutes, obey my ordinances, and keep all my commandments by walking in them, then I will establish my promise with you, which I made to your father David. I will dwell among the children of Israel, and will not forsake my people Israel.' So Solomon built the house, and finished it... The house was finished in all its parts, and according to all its specifications. He was seven years in building it.

David wanted to build a temple to the Lord, but the task fell to his son Solomon. It took seven years, and I find it interesting that Solomon spent the following 13 years building himself a grand palace (1 Kings 7:1). While the temple was being built, however, you would not have experienced a building site as you might today. The absence of noise (1 Kings 6:7) indicates craftsmanship, maybe even worship. Reading the entire chapter offers a glimpse of the enormity and beauty of the structure. Most significant is God's promise to remain with the people as temple construction begins, almost despite the building, rather than because there will now be a 'house of the Lord'.

As with the tabernacle, God's presence is not limited to a particular place, however significant it might be. This can cause tension for many people. I have been saddened by conversations with individuals who did not want to join our congregation on Sundays in the school because, for them, worship can only take place in the ancient church which, at the time, had no roof!

God's words remind us of God's eternal presence and the need to obey God, not places or forms of worship. Yet the regular, weekly gathering of people to encourage one another, to pray, and to sing to and hear from God empowers individuals. A relatively new member of the church brought a friend. Both come on Sundays when circumstances allow. Within the past few months, each has said independently, 'Church stays with me during the week.' In Jesus' words, these people are not far from the kingdom.

Loving God, thank you for places of Christian worship and for all who maintain and treasure them. Teach us to recognise your presence within and beyond the building. Amen

LAKSHMI JEFFREYS

Who and where is God?

'But will God indeed dwell on the earth? Even heaven and the highest heaven cannot contain you, much less this house that I have built! Have regard to your servant's prayer and his plea, O Lord my God, heeding the cry and the prayer that your servant prays to you today; that your eyes may be open night and day towards this house, the place of which you said, "My name shall be there", that you may heed the prayer that your servant prays towards this place... heed and forgive.'

Seven years after the first dressed stone is placed on site, the temple courts are filled with people as the priests place the ark of the covenant in the most holy place. The central holy of holies was surrounded by a larger structure, set within an entrance section. Rooms and courtyards within the areas surrounding the holy of holies varied in purpose. Details are in 1 Kings 6—7 and 2 Chronicles 2—5. Finally, King Solomon offers a magnificent prayer of dedication.

God's name, YHWH (Yahweh), dwelt in the temple. Someone's name established their identity and indicated personality. Calling on the name of a god gave the worshipper access to the god's power and presence. Yahweh's name was not to be manipulated (the first three of the ten commandments). Instead, 'the Name' was bestowed on the temple, to signify God's presence and blessing. This way, God was not located in the temple, but prayers addressed to 'the Name' would be heard by God in heaven. This was crucial for God's people. On the one hand, they could find wholeness and assurance in the temple because God's Name was there. Yet Yahweh was holy, so was not bound to the temple.

The beyond-cosmic God chooses to dwell among the people in the tabernacle, the temple, the person of Jesus. This same God remains with Christians by the Holy Spirit. We have access to the presence and power of God, whose glory filled the temple when Solomon prayed. How might this knowledge inform both our intimate times of prayer and our corporate thanksgiving, intercession, praise and confession?

Take some time to pray Solomon's prayer for yourself, your circumstances and the world around you.

LAKSHMI JEFFREYS

Without God...

Do not trust in these deceptive words: 'This is the temple of the Lord, the temple of the Lord, the temple of the Lord'... Here you are, trusting in deceptive words to no avail. Will you steal, murder, commit adultery, swear falsely, make offerings to Baal, and go after other gods that you have not known, and then come and stand before me in this house, which is called by my name, and say, 'We are safe!' – only to go on doing all these abominations? Has this house, which is called by my name, become a den of robbers in your sight? You know, I too am watching, says the Lord.

'Functional atheism' is a frightening concept. People observe religious rituals with others and perhaps even alone. The 'correct' words are said and actions undertaken, with no thought given to who God is and who we are as God's people. I wept my way through the retreat before I became a church minister, as I began to realise I had abilities to preach, offer pastoral care and even to pray without referencing God. I wonder how often you, as I, have 'gone through the motions' on a Sunday or even reading *New Daylight*: once religious duty is done, I can get on with life, occasionally asking God to bless my plans!

Jeremiah's cries were uttered in the temple courts. Rather than the experience of God's presence, sacrificial worship in the temple had become self-indulgent. God had become what one person called 'a function of a religious enterprise', utterly ignoring God's character to manipulate the system. Both the temple itself and the forms of worship had become idols, as God's people lost sight of their true God. In a few days, we shall explore what happened when Jesus quoted Jeremiah's words as he overthrew the tables in the courtyards. In the meantime, religion easily becomes a means to an end, as religious leaders put status, personal pride, wealth or any number of causes before encounter with the living God. Perhaps I remain in control when I choose ritual over relationship, functional atheism over faith in God.

What might it mean for you today 'to do justice, and to love kindness, and to walk humbly with your God?' (Micah 6:8).

LAKSHMI JEFFREYS

Temple destroyed

O God, why have you rejected us so long? Why is your anger so intense against the sheep of your own pasture? Remember that we are the people you chose long ago, the tribe you redeemed as your own special possession! And remember Jerusalem, your home here on earth. Walk through the awful ruins of the city; see how the enemy has destroyed your sanctuary… They burned your sanctuary to the ground. They defiled the place that bears your name.

It is said that a fish has no concept of water. When we are utterly immersed in something, we have no idea what is really happening. This was the case as God's people increasingly took God's presence for granted and forgot the instructions to keep the commandments. Various kings made alliances with neighbouring countries and adopted their practices, including religious observances. Hezekiah and, later, Josiah made reforms, heeding warnings from the prophets, but they could not undo the damage done by Ahaz and Manasseh. Eventually Nebuchadnezzar of Babylon captured Jerusalem, destroying all the significant buildings, including the temple, and carrying off key people to exile.

The lament of the psalmist is heartfelt. Why has God abandoned us? Yet perhaps the psalmist recalled that, despite the lack of any visible presence, God remained in heaven, as he moves from cries of despair to recollection of God's nature, power and work.

National and international disasters necessarily lead to reflection and lament. The Covid pandemic provoked significant heart-searching, with some people wondering, as we mourned deaths and lost the ability to meet in person for worship, if this was God's punishment. Sadly, countries still experience invasion by neighbouring states, resulting in the destruction of cities and places of worship. Rather than apportion blame, perhaps we can cry out to our God: holy and intimate; compassionate and just; crucified, risen, ascended into heaven and with all who suffer.

Beginning personally, pray for repentance, where pursuit of power, influence, status or material wealth has replaced humble worship and service, that the world may discover God's presence and peace.

LAKSHMI JEFFREYS

My temple will be glorious!

'Foreigners will come to rebuild your towns, and their kings will serve you. For though I have destroyed you in my anger, I will now have mercy on you through my grace. Your gates will stay open day and night to receive the wealth of many lands. The kings of the world will be led as captives in a victory procession. For the nations that refuse to serve you will be destroyed... the forests of cypress, fir, and pine – to beautify my sanctuary. My Temple will be glorious! The descendants of your tormentors... will call you the City of the Lord, and Zion of the Holy One of Israel.'

The rules and regulations about who could do what, when and where in the temple were seemingly endless and related, almost entirely, to God's people. Yet the whole system of the tabernacle and later, the temple, was to witness to and demonstrate life with God on God's terms. Perhaps it is understandable, then, that eventually the temple and the living God would be honoured and worshipped by 'outsiders'.

While Isaiah's words offer a picture of hope for the future, following the exile, they are also for us. We no longer have a temple in Jerusalem (and later this week we will discover that what we have is even better), but we have the opportunity to demonstrate something so magnificent that those who know nothing of God want to be part of the community. They 'see how these Christians love one another' and want a part of it. What a shame, then, that we can become so inward-facing, worried about correct forms of liturgy and music, what people wear, who does what, when and how, and specific interpretations of the Bible, that we lose sight of our purpose.

The most effective way to destroy an enemy is to make them a friend. This was God's plan for humanity – first through the chosen people as they encountered God in the temple; clearly through Jesus; and now through the Holy Spirit at work in, through and around us. This knowledge might inform and transform how we are and 'do' church.

Who belongs to your church and on whose terms? Are 'outsiders' enemies or nearly friends?

LAKSHMI JEFFREYS

A new temple

For thus says the Lord of hosts: Once again, in a little while, I will shake the heavens and the earth and the sea and the dry land; and I will shake all the nations, so that the treasure of all nations shall come, and I will fill this house with splendour, says the Lord of hosts. The silver is mine, and the gold is mine, says the Lord of hosts. The latter splendour of this house shall be greater than the former, says the Lord of hosts; and in this place I will give prosperity, says the Lord of hosts.

Yesterday we read Isaiah's vision of the purpose of the new temple. Today Haggai urges the people to rebuild the structure. After all, they have houses, so God's house should surely be restored. Then God's people can rediscover what might happen if they put God first. Certainly, the image in today's reading is of splendour and magnificence. The difference between this temple and the first is that the king would not be in charge, as Solomon had been. Now it was up to the people, led by God's chosen spokesman, Zerubbabel, to heed the words of the prophets Haggai and Zechariah, to re-establish God's visible rule and presence with God's people.

The problem was that the people were exhausted. They had returned from exile and were unsure about everything. During the aftermath of the pandemic this was the case for almost everyone I met. There was also economic hardship for many and a sense of having to do more with less. One morning I heard about the death of a man – a husband and father – who found everything was too much and felt a failure. Do Haggai's words have anything to say to his widow and family or to other people who have reached the end of their tether?

National and international crises exacerbate personal difficulties, and there are fewer people to share the burden. Christians need to seek the presence and peace of God. This way, we can discover our part as God's people, to live and thereby to share the blessings of the temple.

Remember God's promises and pray for people you know (including yourself if necessary) who need God's presence and peace.

LAKSHMI JEFFREYS

Good news?

Then Jesus entered the temple and drove out all who were selling and buying in the temple, and he overturned the tables of the money-changers and the seats of those who sold doves. He said to them, 'It is written, "My house shall be called a house of prayer"; but you are making it a den of robbers.' The blind and the lame came to him in the temple, and he cured them. But when the chief priests and the scribes saw the amazing things that he did… they became angry.

It does not take long for hierarchy to develop and those in charge to want to be seen to be important. One effective way of boosting morale, at least short-term, is to put other people down or to exclude them. Jesus was incandescent that the very individuals tasked with leading people in the ways of God – who loved everyone created in God's image – were deciding who was 'in' and who was 'out'. They were exploiting people's hope of access to God. How wonderful that, having challenged the system of earning the right to pray, Jesus then heals outcasts – the blind and the lame, who would have no recognised place in society.

You might like rules and regulations: they enable you to feel safe. You might hate them, feeling constrained by anyone or anything telling you how to behave. (A friend this way inclined once confessed to seeing speed limits as guidelines. As more of a rule-keeper, I was horrified!) The temple was designed to allow a huge number of people to encounter the holy God of everything. There had to be systems in place to prevent utter chaos. Unfortunately, the religious leaders had lost sight of whose temple it was. Consequently, people who came were robbed of God's peace and presence, hope and forgiveness, restoration and joy.

It is easy to forget that our faith is one of celebration: we are heralds of good news. God has saved us, through Jesus, to live fully and well and to share well-being with the whole created order. How many churches or Christian organisations are known as agents of joy and celebration?

Bad news sells. Ask God to show you how to be an agent of good news in all your encounters. Practice makes perfect!

LAKSHMI JEFFREYS

Jesus is God's temple

The Jews then said to him, 'What sign can you show us for doing this?' Jesus answered them, 'Destroy this temple, and in three days I will raise it up.' The Jews then said, 'This temple has been under construction for forty-six years, and will you raise it up in three days?' But he was speaking of the temple of his body. After he was raised from the dead, his disciples remembered that he had said this; and they believed the scripture and the word that Jesus had spoken.

Shortly before this passage and as we saw yesterday, Jesus overturned the temple tables, and John's account emphasises that the temple had become a marketplace. Jesus was not condemning the necessary exchange of money and goods to enable sacrifices but declaring, now he was there, that the temple had lost its purpose. The tabernacle and the temple enabled the people to know the presence of God among them. Finally, God was with them in the flesh: the building was obsolete.

Knowing the end of the story, we recognise the significance of 'raising up': first Jesus' body after three days, then his ascension to heaven. The same would be the case for the disciples as they understood Jesus' words and in the light of scripture. Central to Jesus' words and actions in this passage and the preceding verses is Jesus' identity as God's Son, God with the chosen people, bringing light and life to those who believe. Perhaps the difference between then and now is that the disciples in Jesus' day were compelled to live in the light of Jesus' words and actions; 21st-century western Christians have the option to consider the Bible as useful theory or a handbook for life, slightly longer and harder to fathom than other self-help manuals.

Cynical as this statement may seem, is it so far from the truth? Many of us have had experiences of God speaking to us powerfully through the Bible and challenging 'shallow' religion. If Jesus is now the embodiment of the temple, we need to come to him for everything: to celebrate, thank, ask, repent of sin and to be restored to life among God's people.

How does 'Jesus as temple' challenge your prayers and lifestyle?

LAKSHMI JEFFREYS

We are God's temple

Do you not know that you are God's temple and that God's Spirit dwells in you? If anyone destroys God's temple, God will destroy that person. For God's temple is holy, and you are that temple... Do you not know that your body is a temple of the Holy Spirit within you, which you have from God, and that you are not your own? For you were bought with a price; therefore glorify God in your body.

Granted, these two statements are not technically about the temple in Jerusalem or what followed, but they are relevant and worth considering. Both emphasise whose temple it is – God's. In the first, Paul is speaking to the congregation, full of dissension and unkindness. The second is addressed to individuals: while the focus is sexual behaviour, we recognise that everything we do with and to our physical bodies matters.

Christian faith is lived in the material world. The temple was an actual place of sanctuary and holiness, where people learned to conduct every aspect of physical life as God intended. Yesterday we remembered that Jesus was the embodiment of God; the temple was no longer necessary. Following Jesus' death, resurrection and ascension, the Holy Spirit lives in and through Christians: individually and corporately. It might feel as if I am labouring the point, but it can be easy to allow faith to be cerebral, rather than affect our daily lives.

How I behave towards my sister or brother in the church matters, because together we are the dwelling place of God's Holy Spirit. Holy living offers a glimpse of how Jesus lived, demonstrating God's love for the world in every word and action and challenging anyone or anything that does not enhance life. The temple in Jerusalem was the place of God's presence and peace. What needs to change for your church (or mine) to exhibit this in every word and action? Meanwhile, God's Holy Spirit lives in each Christian. How I treat myself – what I put into my body and how I use and move it – shows whether or not I see myself as so valuable that Jesus died for me.

God so loved the whole physical, material world that he sent his Son...

LAKSHMI JEFFREYS

Now and not yet

Now if he were on earth, he would not be a priest at all, since there are priests who offer gifts according to the law. They offer worship in a sanctuary that is a sketch and shadow of the heavenly one; for Moses, when he was about to erect the tent, was warned, 'See that you make everything according to the pattern that was shown you on the mountain.' But Jesus has now obtained a more excellent ministry, and to that degree he is the mediator of a better covenant, which has been enacted through better promises.

It cannot have been easy to be a Hebrew Christian. You were brought up to keep the law in order to maintain your place among God's chosen people. Jesus was the promised Messiah, and you wanted to live according to his teaching. But as a result, you were being persecuted and, to make matters worse, there were no priests and you had no access to the temple to make sacrifices to atone for your sins.

The writer of the letter explains how there was no requirement for sacrifice after Jesus' ultimate sacrifice on the cross. Followers of Jesus were set free from the need to perform actions to put things right with God; all they needed to do was come to God in prayer. Jesus was interceding for them at God's right hand. While persecution was ghastly, they could encourage one another and were empowered by God's Holy Spirit.

Living in the 'between' times is not easy. We have glimpses of heaven, but the world is not as it will be when Christ returns as king. While sacrificial rituals in the temple are unnecessary, perhaps spiritual disciplines help. Daily prayer and study of scripture; honest reflection alone and with trusted Christian friends; time in quiet, contemplating a verse or story from the Bible; habitual acts of service; regular fasting from food, technology or anything else, to focus more fully on God; keeping the sabbath (a day to enjoy God and those you love most) – the list is endless.

Choose a spiritual discipline, perhaps one less familiar to you, and note what happens over the coming days and weeks in your relationship with God as you practise it.

LAKSHMI JEFFREYS

God is the Temple

I saw no temple in the city, for its temple is the Lord God the Almighty and the Lamb. And the city has no need of sun or moon to shine on it, for the glory of God is its light, and its lamp is the Lamb. The nations will walk by its light, and the kings of the earth will bring their glory into it. Its gates will never be shut by day – and there will be no night there. People will bring into it the glory and the honour of the nations. But nothing unclean will enter it, nor anyone who practises abomination or falsehood, but only those who are written in the Lamb's book of life.

Every few years I indulge in 'The Chronicles of Narnia' by C.S. Lewis. The final book in the series, *The Last Battle*, includes a picture of everyone following Aslan 'further up and further in', exploring the land where they belong forever. Just as Jesus was the temple, heralding the 'between times', so, at the end, God will be the temple. Compare the splendour of the picture in Revelation with the details of the tabernacle in Exodus or even Solomon's temple. Little wonder the writer to the Hebrews speaks of a pale imitation.

In the beginning, God promised visibly to be with God's people. In the end, God's people will be physically with God and one another. Worship will be of God and God alone. Jesus has made the ultimate sacrifice and God's glory, presence and peace will be experienced always and forever by everyone present, regardless of nationality, gender or any human distinctions. For now, we need to practise worshipping God with us, rather than physical buildings, rituals, ways of life, possessions, people, or anyone or anything else. When we fail or forget, we can return to Jesus, who has bought us at a price. We are not called in isolation, but alongside one another, that God's glory will be seen by outsiders. Temples might be spectacular, but the focus is the god at the centre. May we learn true Christian worship.

Thank you for your promise to be with your people. Please teach me to live in the light of this promise, that others will see and believe. Amen

LAKSHMI JEFFREYS

Micah

I sometimes find myself challenged by opponents of organised religion who claim that holy texts are outdated and irrelevant. They point at Christianity's adherence to the Bible as a sign that we are concerned with the past rather than the present and criticise what they see as the outdated views contained within scripture. Of course, reading the Old Testament from a modern perspective requires us to be prepared to challenge some behaviours and expectations described in the text that we no longer believe to be accept-able (e.g. slavery), but it is astonishing how little human nature has changed over the millennia.

While we know little about the man who is credited with the prophetic writings contained within the book of Micah, the messages they proclaim remain startlingly pertinent today. Micah speaks powerfully against the misuse of power, examines the distorting effects of wealth and privilege, and describes how greed can lead individuals into debased behaviour. He criticises corrupt politicians and people who misuse the influence they have in order to lead others astray.

Micah's preoccupations have much to say to us. We might consider his comments about false prophets when we think about the impact of social media on the young and the vulnerable. His distaste for those who say what their listeners want to hear so they can make money reminds us to be alert to biased reporting. It is sadly all too easy to see the contemporary relevance of Micah's horror at the waging of war against the peaceful and to weep with him at those who suffer the consequences of evil.

Yet this is not a book of despair. Micah trusts in the God who is intimately involved with the world. He knows that God has had a special relationship with a particular group of people – and consequently, their turning away from faithfulness is particularly painful – but he believes firmly that God is concerned with justice and equity for all. He sees a future when God's word will go out to *all* nations and everyone will live in peace and prosperity. It is an inclusive and generous vision that is filled with hope for Micah's people, and hope for us too. We can learn much from it.

AMANDA BLOOR

Signs of the times

For this I will lament and wail: I will go barefoot and naked; I will make lamentation like the jackals, and mourning like the ostriches. For her wound is incurable. It has come to Judah; it has reached to the gate of my people, to Jerusalem. Tell it not in Gath, weep not at all; in Beth-leaphrah roll yourselves in the dust. Pass on your way, inhabitants of Shaphir, in nakedness and shame; the inhabitants of Zaanan do not come forth.

Sometimes it is easier to see the consequences of our actions by looking at others than it is to examine our own motives. In this passage, the prophet makes it clear that sinfulness leads to judgement, and that judgement has consequences. A series of towns are mentioned, and the implication is that they are suffering as a direct result of their transgressions. They are shamed and grieved beyond tears.

The prophet knows that his own people are no better; a similar fate awaits Judah and Jerusalem. What can he do other than 'lament and wail' the sins which God has witnessed, hoping, perhaps, that there might still be time to change and avert disaster?

We live in a time where our actions can have global consequences and when it is possible, through modern communications, to be instantly aware of events in distant places. Yet we can remain detached and complacent, ready to recognise the failings of others while refusing to accept that we – both as individuals and as a nation – behave in ways which do not fit with our faith. We worry about climate change, for example, or about the exploitation of workers, without paying attention to the involvement of our consumerist desires in these issues. It is all too easy to assume that the fault lies elsewhere, or that it is too big for us to address. Perhaps we, like Micah, need to read the signs of the times and adjust our actions as a result.

Merciful God, forgive us our sins of carelessness, greed and complacency. Give us the desire to change and hearts that are ready to love others more than ourselves. We ask this through your Son, who lived and died for love of us all, Jesus Christ our Lord. Amen

AMANDA BLOOR

Because we can

Alas for those who devise wickedness and evil deeds on their beds! When the morning dawns, they perform it, because it is in their power. They covet fields, and seize them; houses, and take them away; they oppress householder and house, people and their inheritance. Therefore, thus says the Lord: Now, I am devising against this family an evil from which you cannot remove your necks; and you shall not walk haughtily, for it will be an evil time.

If you've ever watched small children playing together, you have probably seen a moment when one of them deliberately antagonises another. One child might tug another's hair in order to produce a reaction or wait until their sibling's back is turned before snatching up a favourite toy. This might be a necessary developmental stage that helps with learning where boundaries lie, or perhaps there is just a human propensity to do something we know is wrong because we think we can get away with it. Just because we can, does not mean we should.

The prophet Micah certainly recognised the link between thinking about bad deeds and doing them. He criticises those who are so proud that they 'walk haughtily' and spend their nights planning theft and oppression. Then in the morning, instead of being ashamed of their dark fantasies, they put them into practice. 'God sees you!' he reminds them, 'and you will be cast down from your arrogance.'

Sadly, human nature has not changed much over the millennia. There are still too many examples of people who wield their power as a weapon rather than using it for good – dictators, plutocrats and political leaders who bolster their own self-esteem by making life miserable for those they consider unworthy of consideration. Yet God sees this and weeps. Freedom will come to those who suffer, and justice will prevail.

Jesus, who loved the poor, the outcast and the rejected, help us to look at the world with your eyes. Make us agents of change, unafraid to stand up for what is right. Fill our hearts with your love and a fierce desire for justice. Amen

AMANDA BLOOR

Banding together

I will surely gather all of you, O Jacob, I will gather the survivors of Israel; I will set them together like sheep in a fold, like a flock in its pasture; it will resound with people. The one who breaks out will go up before them; they will break through and pass the gate, going out by it. Their king will pass on before them, the Lord at their head.

People sometimes say to me, 'I do not go to church; you do not need to go to church to be a Christian.' My response is, 'Yes, but it is much more difficult to be a Christian without the support of others!' We are a family through Christ, and healthy families encourage and help one another. They rejoice with each other when there are things to celebrate, and they offer care when times are hard.

Here, Micah reminds his people that despite their current sufferings, they belong to God. They are not alone and they have not been forgotten. Like sheep feeding happily on good pasture, then safely gathered into the security of a sheepfold, they have the reassurance of company and the hope of freedom, led by the Lord, their shepherd and king. There *is* a better future ahead; they *will* be led out through the gate, their exile at an end.

For Micah's community, it is crucial to remember that, although there has been judgement, there is still hope. God gathers the 'survivors' together so that it is apparent that the people of Israel – the people who, although they have transgressed, are still special to the Lord – can once again be built up. We might find ourselves at times in a similar frame of mind. Tragedies or circumstances are hard to bear alone, but supportive Christian friends can remind us that we are valuable to God. They can help us repent of the things we know we have got wrong and assure us that Christ is ready to forgive. And they can stay with us while we wait for better times to come.

Christ, the good shepherd, may I know that I am never alone. Gather me safely in your sheepfold and lead me into a better future. Amen

AMANDA BLOOR

Loving evil

And I said: Listen, you heads of Jacob and rulers of the house of Israel! Should you not know justice? – you who hate the good and love the evil, who tear the skin off my people, and the flesh off their bones; who eat the flesh of my people, flay their skin off them, break their bones in pieces, and chop them up like meat in a kettle, like flesh in a cauldron.

These are horrifying images. Those who have power and influence are accused of misusing their positions to an outrageous extent. Like a perverted cookery book, the prophet describes how the 'heads and rulers' dismember their people like joints of meat ready for the pot, butcher them with violent lack of care, tear off skin and flesh and eat. It is greedy, disgusting, abhorrent behaviour.

It is most likely that this is meant to be seen as a metaphor rather than reality. Rather than describing real events, Micah is making a point about the misuse of power and the abuse of the judicial system. But the passion with which he paints a picture that is almost too horrible to face reflects the anger he feels. Surely the leaders he criticises must face God's judgement and receive punishment for their actions. Surely justice and righteousness must be restored.

We have too many examples across the centuries of dictators who have moved from oppressing the weak to seeming to revel in seeing how far they can go. The adage that absolute power corrupts absolutely is, sadly, based upon some very real truths. Yet there are examples too of brave men and women who have stood against those who love evil, even at the cost of their own lives. Many have been people of faith.

Jesus is our ultimate exemplar of resisting evil and speaking truth to power. He also paid a heavy price, but he trusted that God would be able to bring light into the heart of darkness. We owe him our freedom and our thanks.

Jesus, lover of the nations, thank you for your steadfastness in the face of violence and fear. Help us to act with courage when we face evil. Give us strength and make us bearers of light. Amen

AMANDA BLOOR

Learning God's ways

In days to come the mountain of the Lord's house shall be established as the highest of the mountains, and shall be raised up above the hills. Peoples shall stream to it, and many nations shall come and say: 'Come, let us go up to the mountain of the Lord, the house of the God of Jacob; that he may teach us his ways and that we may walk in his paths.' For out of Zion shall go forth instruction, and the word of the Lord from Jerusalem.

Here we have a change of tone, moving from the prophet's outrage and anger towards hope and optimism. There won't be an immediate resolution – the changes are for the 'days to come' – but there will be a time when people will return to faithful living and learn God's ways.

It's easy, when caught amid difficulty or sorrow, to become swallowed up by despair that can eat away at our faith. It is no accident that despair was traditionally considered a serious sin, as it implies a lack of trust in God's saving help, but when everything seems to be dark, it is hard to keep a sense of balance. Micah's community have experienced the consequences of their transgressions against God and against each other; they have seen disaster come upon them, and they have suffered greatly. Yet there is hope. There *will* be a time, says the prophet, when 'many nations' will come flocking to God's presence. Peace and order will be restored as their relationship with God is renewed.

Living in hope is arguably one of the most important aspects of a mature spirituality. But hope is not wishy-washy optimism; rather it is the determination to hold fast to a belief that looks for evidence of God's saving love. When we are tempted to fall into despair, we can call to mind the times when God's presence has been very real and when our lives have been shaped and enlarged by our faith. Learning to recognise God's ways is a lifelong and life-enhancing task.

When I am beset by difficulties, Lord, remind me that I have hope. Teach me your ways and help me always to trust in you. Amen

AMANDA BLOOR

War and peace

He shall judge between many peoples, and shall arbitrate between strong nations far away; they shall beat their swords into ploughshares, and their spears into pruning-hooks; nation shall not lift up sword against nation, neither shall they learn war any more; but they shall all sit under their own vines and under their own fig trees, and no one shall make them afraid; for the mouth of the Lord of hosts has spoken.

I love this well-known passage for its beautiful vision of a world in which war has come to an end, the weapons of war have been turned into tools to till the earth and the peoples of the nations sit under the fruiting plants of their own gardens. It is a vision of not just peace, but also plenty – a return to Eden before the Fall.

It is a reminder of God's power to reach across all the nations, even those 'far away'. This land of hope and abundance is for everyone. It is significant that God is described as judge and arbiter between the nations; it suggests that to bring about this new paradise, all people will need to respect God's wisdom and submit to his guidance. If this comes to pass, there truly will be no one to cause fear, because all will wish to live together in peace.

How we wish this day would come! We continue to live in a world where some may enjoy peace while others endure the effects of war. It can be easy to ignore the sufferings of people who are a long way off, but recent military actions in Europe have reminded us that conflict can come very close to home with shocking speed. Without peace for all, there will always be an undercurrent of fear and the possibility of violence. Without learning to live under God's guiding hand, we risk losing the things we value most.

God of righteousness and love, help us to turn away from war. Encourage us to plant and to grow; to build up rather than to cast down; to live in harmony rather than in enmity. We ask this through your Son, our Lord. Amen

AMANDA BLOOR

O little town

But you, O Bethlehem of Ephrathah, who are one of the little clans of Judah, from you shall come forth for me one who is to rule in Israel, whose origin is from of old, from ancient days... And he shall stand and feed his flock in the strength of the Lord, in the majesty of the name of the Lord his God. And they shall live secure, for now he shall be great to the ends of the earth; and he shall be the one of peace.

I wonder what Micah's audience would have thought when they heard this statement of hope? The promise of a good ruler for Israel, one who is guided and strengthened by his relationship with God, might have been encouragement enough. The insistence that this person would be 'great' not just in the immediate locality, but 'to the ends of the earth' might have raised some eyebrows, especially as he is foretold as coming from Bethlehem, that little town of little importance. And yet, Micah is insistent. There will be a king of peace making the future of the world one of plenty and security. It is very good news.

When we read this passage today, we immediately link it with our prince of peace, our good shepherd born in Bethlehem and dismissed by some as being of no importance. The son of a stone and woodworker, the friend of fishermen and fools, Jesus the teacher and healer, who valued peace and justice more than he valued his own safety. Because of him, we, like Micah's listeners, can live secure.

It is easy to overlook what comes out of ordinary places. Yet if we trust in a God who created the whole world and loves it, then we shouldn't be surprised that every part of creation is filled with divine promise. That includes us! However small and insignificant we feel, we too can act 'in the strength of the Lord'. Pray today that each of us lives with that belief.

Loving God, we can feel that we are little people in insignificant places. Help us to trust that you have a task for us and give us the strength we need to carry it out. Amen

AMANDA BLOOR

Tough love

Hear what the Lord says: Rise, plead your case before the mountains, and let the hills hear your voice… for the Lord has a controversy with his people, and he will contend with Israel. 'O my people, what have I done to you? In what have I wearied you? Answer me! For I brought you up from the land of Egypt, and redeemed you from the house of slavery; and I sent before you Moses, Aaron, and Miriam.'

We know that God is all-powerful, and we trust that God is good. It is quite a leap to think of the creator as having feelings that are hurt. Yet here we see God pleading a case against an ungrateful nation and demanding that they explain their behaviour.

'Why have you behaved in this way?' asks God. 'This is what I've done for you!' It is reminiscent of a divorce hearing, with the injured party reminding their spouse of the sacrifices they have made. And, as in all relationships that are struggling, both sides can feel misunderstood.

Of course, God is in the right here. Despite the ways in which the Israelites have benefited from God's care, they have behaved badly and turned away from the one who cares most for them. They have lived corruptly, worshipped false gods and acted violently towards others. They have forgotten the covenant promises made between God and their ancestors and the love that originally bound them together.

Just as human relationships can wither away if neglected, so our relationship with God deserves proper attention. Do we maintain a healthy prayer life? Are we looking for signs of God's presence in the world around us? Are we ready to welcome the stranger as if we welcomed Christ? Do we allow the Holy Spirit into our innermost being, prepared to be changed by the encounter?

God's tough love is designed to bring home the realities of a painful situation. The relationship can be rebuilt, but it will require commitment and work.

I know, Lord, that there are times when I have taken your love for granted.
I have stopped listening to you and turned inwards to my own desires.
Forgive me and bring me back to your presence. Amen

AMANDA BLOOR

All God requires

'With what shall I come before the Lord, and bow myself before God on high? Shall I come before him with burnt-offerings, with calves a year old? Will the Lord be pleased with thousands of rams, with tens of thousands of rivers of oil? Shall I give my firstborn for my transgression, the fruit of my body for the sin of my soul?' He has told you, O mortal, what is good; and what does the Lord require of you but to do justice, and to love kindness, and to walk humbly with your God?'

There is a human tendency to wildly overcompensate when we realise we have behaved badly. We can see that pattern here; following on from God's accusations, there are escalating attempts to put things right. Perhaps burnt offerings will placate God, or oil in such quantities that it flows like rivers. Should a firstborn child be offered to God to mend the relationship? Might a sacrifice of that magnitude be sufficient?

Then comes the crux of the issue. It is not things for which God asks, but qualities: justice, kindness, humility. Simple values that can change the individual, but which also have the capacity to shape whole communities.

It is important to note that these are not abstract goals, but active behaviours. The people are asked to *do*, to *love* and to *walk*. They are expected to live these qualities out, to put them to work in everyday encounters and major decisions alike. If this happens, the wickedness that God has criticised in them will simply stop.

As people of faith and members of faith communities, it can be helpful to use Micah's instructions as the basis of regular audits. Are we applying these standards to our behaviours, as individuals or groups? Would God look and believe that our ways are 'good'?

Merciful God, forgive us for the many times we fail to remember that you call us to do justice, to love kindness and to walk humbly with you. Change our hearts and guide our ways, that we may remember what is right and good. Help us to be your people so that we may confidently affirm that you are our God. Amen

AMANDA BLOOR

Filling the gap

Therefore I have begun to strike you down, making you desolate because of your sins. You shall eat, but not be satisfied, and there shall be a gnawing hunger within you; you shall put away, but not save, and what you save, I will hand over to the sword. You shall sow, but not reap; you shall tread olives, but not anoint yourselves with oil; you shall tread grapes, but not drink wine.

Medieval monks guarded themselves against acedia, the state where nothing mattered and it was hard to make the effort to do anything. Acedia was an attack upon the soul, a spiritual condition as much as a psychological one. The condition that Micah is describing in the passage above is also a spiritual lack, but it is subtly different. Whereas sufferers of acedia cannot bring themselves to do anything, Micah identifies a frantic activity that is worthless. People eat but are still hungry; they hoard but do not save anything of value; they crush grapes and olives but do not benefit from the produce they yield. This is understood as God's punishment upon them because of their sinful behaviour.

It is a terrible punishment to be dissatisfied with everything. I cannot help feeling that we often see this in those who have most in our society and are seen spending their wealth on fast cars, expensive jewellery, designer clothes and endless holidays. Yet these things never seem to bring true happiness or contentment.

God says to those who are to be made 'desolate' that they will become objects of contempt to others. A feeling of worthlessness and emptiness can lead any of us to seek affirmation, often in unhealthy behaviours. Micah tells us firmly that this is not the way. The only thing that truly satisfies is closeness to God and the knowledge that God loves us as we are, rather than because of what we have.

Dear God, there are so many times when I feel worthless or overlooked. I can find myself longing for things and for admiration from those I do not even know. Rebalance me. Restore me. Help me to know what is truly valuable and seek only you and your love. Amen

AMANDA BLOOR

Whom can you trust?

Put no trust in a friend, have no confidence in a loved one; guard the doors of your mouth from her who lies in your embrace; for the son treats the father with contempt, the daughter rises up against her mother, the daughter-in-law against her mother-in-law; your enemies are members of your own household. But as for me, I will look to the Lord, I will wait for the God of my salvation; my God will hear me.

'Blood is thicker than water,' goes the well-known saying, suggesting that family relationships will prove stronger than all other bonds. Micah, in stark contrast, portrays a world in which all relationships, even the closest, have broken down: sons and daughters disdain their parents – a shocking statement in light of the fifth commandment to 'honour your father and your mother' (Exodus 20:12); lovers are not to be trusted; and household members have become enemies. It is all symbolic of a world where 'natural' behaviours have broken down and chaos reigns.

It is always particularly sad when we feel let down by those in whom we had most confidence. It can do lasting damage, shattering our certainties and leaving us unwilling to trust again. Yet Micah suggests a solution: he vows to look to the Lord and to *wait* for God to hear and save him. Although this moment might feel like disaster, holding on to God is the only possible solution. God is reliable and trustworthy.

Yet waiting is hard. Especially when we are in distress, we hope for quick solutions and rapid resolution, so that the pain will come to an end. Micah reminds us that God's time is different to ours and sometimes we have to be patient. Although we might fear that we have been forgotten, it is not so; God is there, and God will come to our aid.

You are closer to me, my God, than all others. You know me through and through; you hear when I cry out to you. Give me readiness to wait upon your saving love, and grace to know that you are always with me. Lord, I look to you in times of trouble. Do not disappoint me, for I have put my trust in you. Amen

AMANDA BLOOR

Compassion and mercy

Who is a God like you, pardoning iniquity and passing over the transgression of the remnant for your possession? He does not retain his anger forever, because he delights in showing clemency. He will again have compassion upon us; he will tread our iniquities under foot. You will cast all our sins into the depths of the sea. You will show faithfulness to Jacob and unswerving loyalty to Abraham, as you have sworn to our ancestors from the days of old.

I wonder if you have ever spoken to someone who has been so damaged by the hurt inflicted upon them that they cannot forgive the perpetrator? Or perhaps you have found it difficult to forgive someone because the person who offended you seems unrepentant?

We can talk quite lightly about finding resolution when relationships break down, by which we often mean discovering a way ahead that suits the needs of all parties concerned. But divorce lawyers and family mediation specialists will point out that this is not easy – it requires commitment and hard work – and sometimes it is simply not possible.

Nevertheless, in the Lord's Prayer we ask to be forgiven 'as we forgive those who trespass against us'. We can feel that we have failed if we cannot forgive, and we can wonder if that means that God will not forgive us our sins.

These last verses of the book of Micah offer encouragement. They affirm faith in a God who 'delights' in being merciful and who will not stay angry. God has sworn to be faithful and loyal and, despite the many failings of Micah's community, God will continue to love them. In wonderful images, God is described as trampling on iniquities and throwing sins into the sea. This is no ignoring of wrongdoing; rather it is a deliberate wiping away of the evidence. With compassion upon human frailty, God offers a fresh start.

Is there someone whom you wish to be able to forgive? Begin today by asking God to forgive you – and believe that you will be forgiven.

God of compassion and mercy, look upon me with kindness. Help me
to ask for your forgiveness and know myself to be forgiven, that I may
in turn forgive others. Amen

AMANDA BLOOR

Enjoy a little luxury: upgrade to *New Daylight deluxe*

Many readers enjoy the compact format of the regular *New Daylight* but more and more people are discovering the advantages of the larger format, premium edition, *New Daylight deluxe*. The pocket-sized version is perfect if you're reading on the move but the larger print, white paper and extra space to write your own notes and comments all make the deluxe edition an attractive alternative and significant upgrade.

Why not try it to see if you like it? You can order single copies at brfonline.org.uk/newdaylightdeluxe

Deluxe actual size:

gladness instead of mourning, the mantle of spirit. They will be called oaks of righteousness to display his glory.

We learn from these verses that gladness is first them' gladness instead of mourning and praise in gift needs to be received, and action is often re gift. For example, receiving a piano is of little us play it. God has blessed us with 'every spiritual but, metaphorically speaking, *we* have to pour o put on and wear the mantle of praise. The Lord

Become a Friend of BRF
and give regularly to support our ministry

We help people of all ages to grow in faith

We encourage and support individual Christians and churches as they serve and resource the changing spiritual needs of communities today.

Through **Anna Chaplaincy**
we're enabling churches to provide
spiritual care to older people

Through **Living Faith**
we're nurturing faith and resourcing
lifelong discipleship

Through **Messy Church**
we're helping churches to reach out
to families

Through **Parenting for Faith**
we're supporting parents as they raise
their children in the Christian faith

Our ministry is only possible because of the generous support of individuals, churches, trusts and gifts in wills.

As we look to the future and make plans, **regular donations make a huge difference** in ensuring we can both start and finish projects well.

By becoming a Friend of BRF and giving regularly to our ministry you are partnering with us in the gospel and helping change lives.

How your gift makes a difference

£2 a month — Helps us to give away **Living Faith** resources via food banks and chaplaincy services

£10 a month — Helps us to support parents and churches running the **Parenting for Faith** course

£5 a month — Helps us to support **Messy Church** volunteers and grow the wider network

£20 a month — Helps us to develop the reach of **Anna Chaplaincy** and improve spiritual care for older people

How to become a Friend of BRF

Online – set up a Direct Debit donation at **brf.org.uk/donate** or find out how to set up a Standing Order at **brf.org.uk/friends**

By post – complete and return the tear-off form opposite to 'Freepost BRF' (*no other address or stamp is needed*)

If you have any questions, or if you want to change your regular donation or stop giving in the future, do get in touch.

Contact the fundraising team

Email: giving@brf.org.uk
Tel: 01235 462305
Post: Fundraising team, BRF, 15 The Chambers,
         Vineyard, Abingdon OX14 3FE

Registered with
FUNDRAISING
REGULATOR

Bible Reading Fellowship (BRF) is a charity (233280) and company limited by guarantee (301324), registered in England and Wales

SHARING OUR VISION – MAKING A ONE-OFF GIFT

I would like to make a donation to support BRF.
Please use my gift for:

☐ Where the need is greatest ☐ Anna Chaplaincy ☐ Living Faith
☐ Messy Church ☐ Parenting for Faith

Title	First name/initials	Surname	
Address			
			Postcode
Email			
Telephone			
Signature			Date

Our ministry is only possible because of the generous support of individuals, churches, trusts and gifts in wills.

Please treat as Gift Aid donations all qualifying gifts of money made (*tick all that apply*)

giftaid it

☐ today, ☐ in the past four years, ☐ and in the future.

I am a UK taxpayer and understand that if I pay less Income Tax and/or Capital Gains Tax in the current tax year than the amount of Gift Aid claimed on all my donations, it is my responsibility to pay any difference.

☐ My donation does not qualify for Gift Aid.

Please notify BRF if you want to cancel this Gift Aid declaration, change your name or home address, or no longer pay sufficient tax on your income and/or capital gains.

You can also give online at **brf.org.uk/donate**, which reduces our administration costs, making your donation go further.

Please complete other side of form ➲

SHARING OUR VISION – MAKING A ONE-OFF GIFT

Please accept my gift of:

☐ £2 ☐ £5 ☐ £10 ☐ £20 Other £ [   ]

by (*delete as appropriate*):

☐ Cheque/Charity Voucher payable to 'BRF'

☐ MasterCard/Visa/Debit card/Charity card

Name on card

Card no. ☐☐☐☐ ☐☐☐☐ ☐☐☐☐ ☐☐☐☐

Expires end ☐M☐M ☐Y☐Y Security code* ☐☐☐ *Last 3 digits on the reverse of the card

Signature	Date

☐ I would like to leave a gift to BRF in my will.
Please send me further information.

☐ I would like to find out about giving a regular gift to BRF.

For help or advice regarding making a gift, please contact our fundraising team +44 (0)1865 462305

Your privacy

We will use your personal data to process this transaction. From time to time we may send you information about the work of BRF that we think may be of interest to you. Our privacy policy is available at **brf.org.uk/privacy**. Please contact us if you wish to discuss your mailing preferences.

Registered with
FUNDRAISING **REGULATOR**

 Please complete other side of form

Please return this form to 'Freepost BRF'
No other address information or stamp is needed

Bible Reading Fellowship is a charity (233280) and company limited by guarantee (301324), registered in England and Wales

Overleaf... Reading *New Daylight* in a group | Author profile | Recommended reading | Order and subscription forms

Reading *New Daylight* in a group

GORDON GILES

In the Rule of Benedict, which formed the spiritual foundations of the daily prayer life of so many ecclesiastical foundations, daily reading was a key aspect of the community life of work and prayer. The distinct disciplines of reading scripture alone and reading together were both significant in the spiritual and moral formation of the monks of all ranks. With these daily Bible reading notes, we offer scripture and reflective material for personal reading. Yet discussion or shared reflection on the passages chosen and the comments made can also be rewarding, so we also offer some open questions that may enable discussion in a Bible study or other group who gather to take further what is published here. The same questions may also aid personal devotion. Use them as you wish, and may God bless and inspire you on your journey as you read holy words and ponder them in your heart.

General discussion starters

These can be used for any study series within this issue. Remember there are no right or wrong answers – these questions are simply to enable a group to engage in conversation.

- What do you think is the main idea or theme of the author in this series? Did that come across strongly?

- Have any of the issues discussed touched on personal – or shared – aspects of your life?

- What evidence or stories do the authors draw on to illuminate, or be illuminated by, the passages of scripture.

- Which do you prefer: scripture informing daily modern life, or modern life shining a new light on scripture?

- Does the author 'call you to action' in a realistic and achievable way? Do you think their ideas will work in the secular world?

- Have any specific passages struck you personally? If so, how and why? Is God speaking to you through scripture and reflection?

- Was anything completely new to you? Were there any 'eureka' or jaw-dropping moments? If so, what difference will that make?

Questions for specific series
Psalms 15—29 (Elizabeth Rundle)

- Psalms were – and still are – for worshipping God. How does it feel to *study* them? In what ways are they different to other forms of scripture?
- Which of these psalms discussed is your favourite and why?
- Share, reflect on, even sing the psalms we still sing, as hymns, songs, chants, etc. What is it that makes them enduring and ever-relevant?
- What are the different kinds of psalms, the purposes for which they were written? Do they still serve that purpose well today?
- If you were writing a psalm today, what would you praise God for, ask God for, lament or rejoice in?

The upper room (Gordon Giles)

- Think of a place you know where different, significant events have happened. It could be a church, house, public venue or theatre. Share those events.
- Can there be a 'spirit of place' somewhere – what might that mean?
- 'If the walls could talk', what would the walls of the upper room say to us about what they had seen?
- Does it matter where significant events happen, or is it just the events themselves and their meaning and implications that matter? Is it a shame that we cannot be sure where the upper room is now?
- Where is God?

1 Corinthians 11—14 (Naomi Starkey)

- What do you know about first-century Corinth? Can it be equated with anywhere today? What are the similarities and the differences?
- How close to Paul's original description of the Eucharist is what you are used to? Do embellishments, additions and ritual add to or detract from the original early celebrations of Communion?
- What does it mean to both *be* the body of Christ, as members together, and to *eat and drink* the body and blood of Jesus? How do we connect these meanings of the word 'body'?

- Is music a spiritual gift? Are there other (modern) spiritual gifts you might add to Paul's list?
- Are faith, hope and love still the greatest things? What *is* love? Would you adapt Paul's description in any way or is it incapable of improvement?

Micah (Amanda Bloor)

- Amanda Bloor says human nature has changed little over millennia. Do you agree? Are people now 'better' than we were in the past? In what ways are we (or are we not)?
- Can you relate Micah's situation to our own world today? How does that make you feel?
- Where can you see hope in or for the world today?
- What is it to love in hope?
- How can you personally do justice, love kindness and walk humbly with your God? How does society need to change, in communities, governments, nations?
- What is the God we meet in Micah like? What similarities are there between God here and in the Lord's Prayer?

Meet the author: Lakshmi Jeffries

Tell us how you became a Christian.

My parents were Hindus from different parts of India, who met and married in England. In fact, to say my parents were Indian would be the equivalent of having a Swedish mother and Greek father and saying my parents were European – they spoke different Indian languages, ate different food and so on, but both were educated in English and were from the same Hindu caste. When they decided to settle in England with my siblings and I, they encouraged us to take part in all lessons, including Christian RE. As a Brownie, I occasionally read the Bible passage in church on 'Parade Sunday'. My parents felt that all religions taught the same thing about God and, whatever the form, all religions were variations of Hinduism, the oldest religion.

During my final year at school, I became fascinated by Jesus, possibly as a result of something I heard in assembly. My parents encouraged me to explore different faiths, and I loved aspects of Judaism, Buddhism and even bits of Islam, but I kept returning to Jesus. Conversations with Christian friends and a teacher who was also a Christian helped me to conclude that either Jesus was who he claimed to be or he was not. (I had not yet encountered C.S. Lewis' 'mad, bad or God' argument, but it was similar.) On a Thursday afternoon, a few weeks after my 18th birthday, I prayed with the teacher and a local vicar and became a Christian. It was a cerebral rather than emotional occasion, but the emotions came thick and fast soon afterwards!

My parents initially thought I would be Jewish on Friday, Buddhist over the weekend and return to Hinduism by Monday. When this proved not to be the case, they were anxious that I had been brainwashed by a cult. Finally, they told me I could believe what I wanted but I was not to influence my siblings. As a result, I have only answered questions and never proselytised. From the very beginning, I knew that my role was to be faithful to Jesus and that God would be faithful to those I loved most. By the time I felt called to be ordained in the Church of England, my parents and my siblings were hugely encouraging and have supported me ever since.

Shortly before each of my parents died, I had the privilege of praying with them. (My father was unconscious but I prayed with him and his Christian carer and both of us watched him rest more peacefully immediately afterwards.) God remained faithful to them and to me and I am immensely thankful for my upbringing and faith journey.

Who or what have been some of the most significant influences on your Christian journey?

There have been so many people and God-filled circumstances! The teacher who first prayed with me belonged to a house group at her church. In my final year at university, nearly four years after coming to faith, I met a first-year student from that teacher's church. The parents of the student ran the home group in which the teacher – and the student and her parents – had prayed for me each week all those years before. I arrived at a church at the same time as the new assistant minister – whom I had known since he was at training college. He encouraged me to consider ordained ministry, became one of my lecturers and, with his wife, has remained a friend for nearly 40 years. Then there was the time I mislaid my passport in transit in Egypt, on route to Kenya, where I was due to spend a month. Ask me some time about Noah's ark and explaining penguins to a young Muslim official carrying a gun! I have discovered much about God's call and equipping in every aspect of life.

Tell us the current context of your ministry in the church?

Our church is an ancient building in what, perhaps 45 years ago, was a village numbering about 2,000 inhabitants and is now a conurbation with about 15,000 people. Perhaps the Christian song most needed is 'Faithful One, so unchanging', as locals wrestle with huge upheaval in their environment as well as the aftermath of global pandemics, economic recession, etc. We would do well to call out to God again and again.

If you could change one thing in the world what would it be?

If I could change one thing in the world, people would allow themselves and everyone else to make mistakes, get things wrong, and mess up time and again. This would remind us to be human and recognise God as God and might even lead to forgiveness! It is based on an idea highlighted by Henri Nouwen – we need to learn to forgive those we love most (and ourselves) for not being God and therefore hurting us.

Recommended reading

There are no simple answers to life's challenges, so how do we integrate our most testing experiences into our faith in a way which strengthens rather than weakens it? When we are at our weakest, when we feel we most need God and yet have no idea how to talk to him, it is the Psalms which leap to our rescue. With the psalmists as our guides, we learn to draw closer to God, to hear his voice in fresh ways, and to identify what it is that troubles us. Borrowing their words, we find that we are able to articulate our most painful feelings and walk through suffering with honesty, hope, and confidence in the God who travels beside us. *World Turned Upside Down* is an opportunity to read the Psalms differently: an invitation to embark on a new journey.

The following is an edited extract taken from a section entitled 'The elephant in the church', in Chapter 1, 'Making sense of life'.

Living in a world which has long sought to dull and deny pain, it seems natural, when we find ourselves nonetheless assailed by the slings and arrows of outrageous fortune, to turn to the church for help and support. And yet all too often we find that it isn't only our culture which urges us to believe that all is well; we bring our collective inclination to retreat into denial into the church as well. Gathering in beautiful buildings on Sundays, we sing heart-warming songs and uplifting hymns; we repeat comforting liturgical words and remind ourselves what we believe through the taking of bread and wine; we listen to a short talk and pray for those who suffer in distant places. Then we go home, taking our own doubts and difficulties with us. As biblical scholar Walter Brueggemann remarks, it's as if we believe that having faith means a refusal to acknowledge and embrace negativity; as if that would be some kind of failure. So we sing brightly and sometimes beautifully, offer one another coffee and biscuits, and go home slightly more cheerful, hoping that by pretending all is well it will become so.

And yet two things are true. The first is that one of our responsibilities as the church is to help people navigate life, not as we would like it to be, but as it actually is. And the second is that pain lies at the very heart of our faith: in encountering Jesus, we encounter a man who gathered the suffering of the world into his own suffering, who forged a path from death to life, and who through it all earned the right to offer the uniquely powerful invitation 'Come to me, all you who are weary and burdened, and I will give you rest.' Pain is the inescapable thorn in the flesh of the human condition, and an essential element in the journey of every single one of us towards God. Without pain, we cannot grow; pain is the tunnel through which we must pass if we are to reach the light at the other end. Everything depends on how we respond, and how we help others to respond. Many, at the very point when they most need to connect with God, give up on their faith altogether. Overcome by the darkness of the valley, they never reach the green pastures or rest by the refreshing waters. 'What are you going to write about?' asked an old and wise friend. 'Pain,' I replied. 'Thank God,' she said.

Every morning I read the biblical passages set for the day in the Anglican lectionary, and for the past few years I have focused on the Psalms. And in the Psalms too I have found elephants – not the grey, invisible elephants which mope their way silently through our 21st-century world and hide behind the pillars of our churches, but attention-seeking, violently coloured, lambastingly noisy ones. These elephants cannot be ignored; their trumpeting and bellowing echoes from the first psalm to the last, and they rampage with the energy of animals unrestrained in their expression of pain, of anger, of lament and finally of joy. It's said that an elephant can be heard at a distance of six miles; there is so much sheer power wrapped up in the vocalisation of an elephant that I began to pick up my Bible with a newly cautious reverence. Few people know that the elephants are there, lumbering about inside.

And yet so often we don't pray the very psalms which could most help us. 'Which psalms do I know best?', I asked myself as I began to pray my way through them. The 'nice' ones, of course. Psalm 139 probably tops the list – God made me and knows me. Psalm 46, perhaps – 'Be still, and know that I am God.' Psalm 23, of course, with its first-impression promise of green pastures. And the summer cheerfulness of Psalm 104, which sees God stretching out the heavens like a tent, renewing the face of the earth. In these psalms the elephants graze peacefully in a sunlit savannah, and all is well with the world. And yet closer examination reveals that even in these uplifting verses there is an undercurrent of anger and fear.

To order a copy of this book, please use the order form opposite or visit **brfonline.org.uk**

⊃ order

Delivery times within the UK are normally 15 working days. Prices are correct at the time of going to press but may change without prior notice.

tle	Price	Qty	Total
ble in Ten	£12.99		
orld Turned Upside Down	£12.99		
is Crown of Comfort	£9.99		

POSTAGE AND PACKING CHARGES			
er value	UK	Europe	Rest of world
der £7.00	£2.00		
00–£29.99	£3.00	Available on request	Available on request
.00 and over	FREE		

Total value of books	
Postage and packing	
Donation*	
Total for this order	

* Please complete and return the Gift Aid declaration on page 143.

ase complete in BLOCK CAPITALS

tle _____ First name/initials _____ Surname_____

ddress_____

_____ Postcode _____

c. No. _____ Telephone _____

mail_____

ethod of payment

◻ Cheque (made payable to BRF) ◻ MasterCard / Visa

rd no. ▢▢▢▢ ▢▢▢▢ ▢▢▢▢ ▢▢▢▢ ▢▢▢▢

pires end ▢ M ▢ M ▢ Y ▢ Y   Security code ▢▢▢   Last 3 digits on the reverse of the card

will use your personal data to process this order. From time to time we may send you information t the work of BRF. Please contact us if you wish to discuss your mailing preferences **brf.org.uk/privacy**

se return this form to:

15 The Chambers, Vineyard, Abingdon OX14 3FE | **enquiries@brf.org.uk**
erms and cancellation information, please visit **brfonline.org.uk/terms**.

Bible Reading Fellowship (BRF) is a charity (233280) and company limited by guarantee (301324), registered in England and Wales

Bringing people together

'For where two or three gather in my name, there am I with them.'
MATTHEW 18:20 (NIV)

After the events of the past few years the privilege of being able to gather together has never felt more apparent. Whether it be for church services, concerts, sports matches, picnics or all manner of other activities, even the most introverted among us can experience the joy of being together with others.

Our ministries have always brought people together in the name of Jesus: Messy Churches bring the families of their communities under one roof; parents and church leaders meet together to take a Parenting for Faith course; Anna Chaplains bring companionship and support to older people experiencing loneliness. Our Living Faith resources also bring people together, a community of people reading the same Bible notes across the globe – not to mention events like the Festival of Prayer.

As always, BRF adapts to help even more people encounter Jesus, with more and more opportunities to meet in new ways: Messy Church Goes Wild taking their families outside, Messy Church and Parenting for Faith Facebook Live sessions, a community of podcast listeners, online Holy Habits courses and still more. It is a real privilege to be able to create spaces and communities where people can gather and thus be with Jesus.

We want to keep building on the work of the past 100 years, adapting and growing and finding even more glorious ways for people to grow in their faith as individuals and communities.

Our work would not be possible without kind donations from individuals, charitable trusts and gifts in wills. If you would like to support BRF's work now and in the future you can become a Friend of BRF by making a monthly gift of £2 a month or more. We thank you for your friendship.

Find out more at **brf.org.uk/donate**

Judith Moore
Fundraising development officer

Please note our new subscription rates, current until 30 April 2024:

Individual subscriptions
covering 3 issues for under 5 copies, payable in advance
(including postage & packing):

	UK	Europe	Rest of world
New Daylight	£19.05	£26.55	£30.45
New Daylight 3-year subscription (9 issues) (not available for Deluxe)	£54.45	N/A	N/A
New Daylight Deluxe per set of 3 issues p.a.	£24.15	£33.00	£39.00

Group subscriptions
covering 3 issues for 5 copies or more, sent to one UK address (post free):

New Daylight	£14.85 per set of 3 issues p.a.
New Daylight Deluxe	£18.75 per set of 3 issues p.a.

Please note that the annual billing period for group subscriptions runs from 1 May to 30 April.

Overseas group subscription rates
Available on request. Please email **enquiries@brf.org.uk**.

Copies may also be obtained from Christian bookshops:

New Daylight	£4.95 per copy
New Daylight Deluxe	£6.25 per copy

> All our Bible reading notes can be ordered online
> by visiting **brfonline.org.uk/subscriptions**
>
> *New Daylight* is also available as an
> app for Android, iPhone and iPad
> **brfonline.org.uk/apps**

NEW DAYLIGHT INDIVIDUAL SUBSCRIPTION FORM

All our Bible reading notes can be ordered online by visiting
brfonline.org.uk/subscriptions

Title _____ First name/initials _____ Surname _____

Address _____

_____ Postcode _____

Telephone _____ Email _____

Please send *New Daylight* beginning with the September 2023 / January 2024 / May 2024 issue (*delete as appropriate*):

(*please tick box*)	UK	Europe	Rest of world
New Daylight 1-year subscription	☐ £19.05	☐ £26.55	☐ £30.45
New Daylight 3-year subscription	☐ £54.45	N/A	N/A
New Daylight Deluxe	☐ £24.15	☐ £33.00	☐ £39.00

Optional donation* to support the work of BRF £ _____

Total enclosed £ _____ (cheques should be made payable to 'BRF')

* Please complete and return the Gift Aid declaration on page 143 to make your donation even more valuable to us.

Please charge my MasterCard / Visa with £ _____

Card no. ☐☐☐☐ ☐☐☐☐ ☐☐☐☐ ☐☐☐☐

Expires end ☐☐ ☐☐   Security code ☐☐☐   Last 3 digits on the reverse of the card

To set up a Direct Debit, please complete the Direct Debit instruction on page 159.

We will use your personal data to process this order. From time to time we may send you information about the work of BRF. Please contact us if you wish to discuss your mailing preferences **brf.org.uk/privacy**

Please return this form with the appropriate payment to:
BRF, 15 The Chambers, Vineyard, Abingdon OX14 3FE
For terms and cancellation information, please visit **brfonline.org.uk/terms**.

Bible Reading Fellowship is a charity (233280) and company limited by guarantee (301324), registered in England and Wales

ND0223

NEW DAYLIGHT GIFT SUBSCRIPTION FORM

☐ I would like to give a gift subscription (please provide both names and addresses):

Title _____ First name/initials _____ Surname _____

Address _____

_____ Postcode _____

Telephone _____ Email _____

Gift subscription name _____

Gift subscription address _____

_____ Postcode _____

Gift message (20 words max. or include your own gift card):

_____

_____

Please send *New Daylight* beginning with the September 2023 / January 2024 / May 2024 issue (*delete as appropriate*):

(*please tick box*)

	UK	Europe	Rest of world
New Daylight 1-year subscription	☐ £19.05	☐ £26.55	☐ £30.45
New Daylight 3-year subscription	☐ £54.45	N/A	N/A
New Daylight Deluxe	☐ £24.15	☐ £33.00	☐ £39.00

Optional donation* to support the work of BRF £ _____

Total enclosed £ _____ (cheques should be made payable to 'BRF')

* Please complete and return the Gift Aid declaration on page 143 to make your donation even more valuable to us.

Please charge my MasterCard / Visa with £ _____

Card no. ☐☐☐☐ ☐☐☐☐ ☐☐☐☐ ☐☐☐☐

Expires end ☐☐ ☐☐ Security code ☐☐☐ Last 3 digits on the reverse of the card

To set up a Direct Debit, please complete the Direct Debit instruction on page 159.

We will use your personal data to process this order. From time to time we may send you information about the work of BRF. Please contact us if you wish to discuss your mailing preferences **brf.org.uk/privacy**

Please return this form with the appropriate payment to:
BRF, 15 The Chambers, Vineyard, Abingdon OX14 3FE
For terms and cancellation information, please visit **brfonline.org.uk/terms**.

BRF

Bible Reading Fellowship is a charity (233280) and company limited by guarantee (301324), registered in England and Wales

You can pay for your annual subscription to our Bible reading notes using Direct Debit. You need only give your bank details once, and the payment is made automatically every year until you cancel it. If you would like to pay by Direct Debit, please use the form opposite, entering your BRF account number under 'Reference number'.

You are fully covered by the Direct Debit Guarantee:

The Direct Debit Guarantee

- This Guarantee is offered by all banks and building societies that accept instructions to pay Direct Debits.

- If there are any changes to the amount, date or frequency of your Direct Debit, Bible Reading Fellowship will notify you 10 working days in advance of your account being debited or as otherwise agreed. If you request Bible Reading Fellowship to collect a payment, confirmation of the amount and date will be given to you at the time of the request.

- If an error is made in the payment of your Direct Debit, by Bible Reading Fellowship or your bank or building society, you are entitled to a full and immediate refund of the amount paid from your bank or building society.

- If you receive a refund you are not entitled to, you must pay it back when Bible Reading Fellowship asks you to.

- You can cancel a Direct Debit at any time by simply contacting your bank or building society. Written confirmation may be required. Please also notify us.

Instruction to your bank or building society to pay by Direct Debit

Please fill in the whole form using a ballpoint pen and return with order form to:
BRF, 15 The Chambers, Vineyard, Abingdon OX14 3FE

Service User Number: | 5 | 5 | 8 | 2 | 2 | 9 |

Name and full postal address of your bank or building society

To: The Manager	Bank/Building Society
Address	
	Postcode

Name(s) of account holder(s)

Branch sort code

| | | | - | | | | - | | | |

Bank/Building Society account number

| | | | | | | | | |

Reference number

| | | | | | | | |

Instruction to your Bank/Building Society

Please pay Bible Reading Fellowship Direct Debits from the account detailed in this instruction, subject to the safeguards assured by the Direct Debit Guarantee. I understand that this instruction may remain with Bible Reading Fellowship and, if so, details will be passed electronically to my bank/building society.

Signature(s)

Banks and Building Societies may not accept Direct Debit instructions for some types of account.

ND0223

Enabling all ages to grow in faith

Anna Chaplaincy
Living Faith
Messy Church
Parenting for Faith

BRF is a Christian charity that resources individuals and churches. Our vision is to enable people of all ages to grow in faith and understanding of the Bible and to see more people equipped to exercise their gifts in leadership and ministry.

To find out more about our work, visit
brf.org.uk